D0427546

PUT ME IN, COACH

A PARENT'S GUIDE

TO WINNING THE GAME OF

COLLEGE RECRUITING

LAURIE A. RICHTER

RIGHT
FIT
PRESS
Riverwoods, Ilinois

Put Me In, Coach!
A Parent's Guide to Winning the Game of College Recruiting
By Laurie A. Richter

Published by:

RIGHT FIT PRESS   2033 Milwaukee Avenue
Suite 203
Riverwoods, IL 60015

Publisher's Cataloging-In-Publication Data
(Prepared by The Donohue Group, Inc.)

Richter, Laurie A.
   Put me in, Coach : a parent's guide to winning the game of college recruiting / Laurie A. Richter.

   p. ; cm.

   Includes bibliographical references and index.
   ISBN: 978-0-615-21333-0

1. College athletes—Recruiting—United States. 2. Sports—Scholarships, fellowships, etc.— United States. 3. College choice—United States. 4. Students—Recruiting—United States. I. Title.

GV350.5 .R52 2009
796/.071   2008932656

Book and cover design by Peri Poloni-Gabriel, www.knockoutbooks.com

Edited by Gail M. Kearns, To Press and Beyond, www.topressandbeyond.com

Book production coordinated by To Press and Beyond

Printed in the United States of America

TABLE OF CONTENTS

Preface 5

Introduction 7

PART ONE: Where Do You Begin?

CHAPTER 1: Building the Parent/Child Team............................ 13

CHAPTER 2: Is Pursuing a College Sport the Right Decision? 17

PART TWO: Creating Your College List and Finding the Right Fit

CHAPTER 3: Athletic Skill Assessment 27

CHAPTER 4: Perceived Role on the Team 43

CHAPTER 5: Academic Credentials 49

CHAPTER 6: Athletics vs. Academics Priority 61

CHAPTER 7: Non-Athletic College Priorities.............................. 67

CHAPTER 8: Money Concerns.. 73

CHAPTER 9: Two Final Litmus Tests for Your College List................ 91

CHAPTER 10: Starting the Recruiting Process.............................. 97

PART THREE: Getting Coaches Interested

CHAPTER 11: Who Does What?.. 107

CHAPTER 12: Marketing Your Child 113

PART FOUR: Getting Recruited

CHAPTER 13: The Dance Begins 135

CHAPTER 14: The Campus Visit... 149

PART FIVE: Making the Decision

CHAPTER 15: Deciding Which Offer Is Best 163

CHAPTER 16: When Do You Make the Final Decision 171

CHAPTER 17: Creating a Backup Plan.................................... 181

Acknowledgments... 187

Appendix A: D-III Conferences and Links to Their Websites 189

Appendix B: 2008 NCAA Basketball Attendance........... 191

Glossary 197

References 201

Index 203

PREFACE

I recently attended a high school graduation party for a friend's daughter. The hostess knew I was writing a book about college sports recruiting, so the minute I walked through the door she introduced me to a couple whose son was a talented gymnast. He would be a senior in the fall and had taken third place at the state championship his junior year. He wanted to continue competing in college but coaches weren't exactly knocking at the door. The mother, in particular, spoke with a sense of urgency and frustration that I have heard before from many parents of high school athletes. She wasn't sure how to help her son through the recruiting process, and no one was stepping in to lend a helping hand. She knew that time was running out. Her son's excitement and high hopes were giving way to the fear that he might never be part of a college team.

I am a parent—just like those parents—and just like you. Our son, Dylan, was a good student whose dream was to play basketball in college. His junior year rolled around and it was time to start looking at schools. My husband and I wanted him to have the best experience possible—academically, socially, and athletically. How could we put all of these factors into an equation to help him find a college that would be right for him? We learned quickly that the student-athlete's search was much more involved than it was for other kids. Was Dylan a good enough basketball player to play at the college level? Would he fit best in Division I, II, or III? Could he get a scholarship? Could he handle both the academics and play a sport? How could he make sure the right coaches saw him? That he would get playing time? What were his chances of being accepted by his top choices?

Thousands of kids are recruited to play college sports every year. So why did we feel so isolated and unprepared? I am a market researcher by trade, so I did what I was trained to do. I searched the bookstores and online for information that would help Dylan find the right college with athletics as a priority and, just as important, how to survive the process. There was very little. I also spoke with parents whose kids had gone through the recruiting process. There were a handful of happy endings, but there were many more stories filled with frustration, miscommunication, over-inflated expectations, and dashed hopes.

Every year, hundreds of thousands of high school athletes hope to play their sport in college. Most will find the recruiting process complex, frustrating, exhausting, and shrouded in mystery. **It doesn't need to be this way for your child.** When I compared athletes who had positive outcomes with those less satisfied, the difference was seldom due to the level of talent. More often, success came when kids and parents understood the recruiting process, took the initiative to get the athlete noticed, and identified the schools that were the best fit in all areas—not just athletics.

I decided to write this book quite simply because it was the book I wished I had found on the shelf when my son started looking at colleges. The recruiting vignettes are all true. They are the stories of friends, neighbors, extended family, schoolmates, and teammates. Boys and girls that play a wide range of sports. All who had dreams of being recruited to play in college.

Put Me In, Coach is intended for students and the parents of all students who want to play college sports, in any division, with or without an athletic scholarship. My goal is to give you the information and inspiration you need to guide your student-athlete toward a happy ending. May you enter the world of college recruiting with equal doses of realism and optimism.

INTRODUCTION

Spring break means one thing to many families of high school juniors: it's time to start looking at colleges. We started at the University of Michigan, a Big Ten school with over twenty-five thousand undergraduate students. After a long day of touring the campus, I asked my son what he thought. Without hesitation he replied, "It's cool, but I could never play basketball here so let's just go." We knew right then there was no point visiting colleges where our son could not play the sport he loved.

Welcome to the world of the student-athlete. Playing a college sport can be enormously rewarding for your child, but it definitely complicates the search process. All parents want to see their children at a school where they will have every opportunity to learn, mature, and be well prepared for the next stage of life. But prospective college athletes face the challenge of incorporating athletics into this search. While their friends are making their college visits and narrowing their lists, they may be paralyzed by this additional task. It will test their commitment to their sport and their patience—and undoubtedly their parents, too.

The reality is that very few high school athletes will play their sport in college. Just in case you gloss over this now, I will provide actual numbers for you later. I'm hoping you won't ignore this reality twice. Why am I starting here? Because the main premise of this book is that your child will have a better college experience—academic and athletic—if you do a good job upfront of realistically assessing their skills and target your search accordingly. Too often egos get in the way, and I'm not just talking about the student-athlete's. You will be well-served to rid yourself of any preconceived notions about which programs are "worthy" of your child and which aren't. And before you go any further, you should probably decide if this is a book that can help you and your child in this search. You'll know the answer after reading the following two scenarios.

Scenario 1: Your kid is a stud.

There is no one even close. Your child dominates at the high school level and in off-season competition, too. There has been college interest for a while, and from schools you have actually heard of. ***Put this book down now.*** Handlers who will eagerly usher you through the recruiting process will surround you.

Scenario 2: Your kid is a good athlete.

Your child is better than most at the high school level and has received form letters and a few generic e-mails from colleges—perhaps even gotten a few coach calls from schools with smaller programs. But college coaches aren't exactly lining up at the door. **If this is your situation, this book is for you.**

What do you do if you have a kid who is deeply passionate about his sport and can't imagine a college experience without it? The good news is that if that passion is complemented by a reasonable amount of talent, s/he has two of the three essentials s/he needs to compete in college. The third is your help. It's rumored that 90 percent of the attention of college coaches goes to 10 percent of the athletes. But I am convinced there's a roster spot out there for most athletes, so grab this book, roll up your sleeves, and make sure your child hits the recruiting radar.

So how do you make it happen? I begin this book with the first critical step: forging a partnership with your child. You both need to take a good hard look at the question of whether playing college sports is the right decision. If the answer is yes, it's time to identify the characteristics your child is looking for in a college experience. I target six dimensions you can use to create a list of possible choices, highlighting the importance of each to the college search and how they relate to the recruiting process.

Then it's all about the marketing. Your son might be an extremely talented athlete, but have the coaches at his target schools ever seen him compete? Do they know anything about your daughter or her high school program? How should you go about getting in touch with them and what are they looking for? I decided to go straight to the coaches from a variety of sports and schools to ask them how they go about recruiting players—where they look and what gets their attention. You will find their comments and suggestions throughout the book.

And speaking of college coaches, remember this: student-athletes and college coaches are not adversaries. They are allies with a shared objective— to find the best overall college fit for your child. When students end up at the right schools, they will be successful academically *and* athletically and this will reflect positively on the coach. There are unsavory characters in every walk of life, but oftentimes parents who characterize coaches as unethical or dishonest just didn't understand the recruiting process or the constraints that a coach faces.

My hope is that you will arm yourself with *Put Me In, Coach* from the time you start your recruiting journey until you and your child make the final decision. Be diligent, realistic, and always keep an open mind. A coach from a school you never heard of just might have the program you were looking for all along. You will have done your homework, so you will recognize the best fit—and it will undoubtedly come back to the reason your child wanted to compete in college in the first place: for the love of the game.

Once the preseason starts, it doesn't matter if you're at an Ivy League school or a neighborhood JUCO (junior college), or if you got your big scholarship or not. The reputation of the school and the money some coach may give you could have almost NOTHING to do with the quality of your experience. The same four things that are making you happy now as an athlete will make you happy in college:

1. *I'm actually playing a lot and in the lineup often.*
2. *The level of play is good enough.*
3. *The team is successful in its conference or league.*
4. *The coaches know me well and I trust their judgment.*

Brian Parker, Head Coach, Women's Soccer, Frostburg State University

---

PART ONE

Where Do You Begin?

CHAPTER 1

BUILDING THE PARENT/CHILD TEAM

Here is an unexpected benefit of the recruiting process: it provides you and your child with an opportunity to become closer by working together on what may be the last really big decision you make together before s/he heads out into the world beyond your doorstep. But make no mistake, it will present challenges and frustrations before you reach your final, collective decision and it can put a lot of strain on the parent/child relationship. The college search process is stressful enough and adding the sports dimension to it just adds another layer of complication. Let me try to anticipate some of these challenges for you. Parents and a sixteen- or seventeen-year-old are not the ideal pairing in terms of communication. Your goal should be to talk your way through this and still be talking at the end. We all have a tendency to fall back into long-established patterns of behavior without even realizing it, and they can really stymie communication. A couple of suggestions even though they seem deceptively simplistic:

> Listen to your child's point of view. You don't have to agree and you don't have to like it, but s/he does have the right to express it, and you should respect where s/he is coming from. Ask your kid for their rationale and be prepared to offer your own. You are long past the years of "because I said so" or "because I'm the parent."

> **Be honest about constraints.** Kids need to enter this process with a full understanding of what the starting point is. If there are deal breakers, you need to let them know. For example, if you won't let them go more than five hundred miles from home, let them know that at the onset. For many families, cost can be a serious constraint as well.

> **Have a discussion about what each of your roles will be.** There is no easy answer and books that tell you who should be doing what are misguided. Kids move to the beat of their own drum. I have two kids, and going through this process with each of them would be very different. Find a way that works; just make sure you discuss it and agree upon it.

Be honest with each other (and yourself) about your agendas and biases, and see if you can find some common ground. Oftentimes, these only become apparent as the process unfolds. Both parties can have blinders on in the heat of battle. Here are some examples of mismatched agendas that I heard when I compared notes with other families:

1. The parents want their kid focused primarily on academics; the kid wants to focus on the sport but is willing to take a few classes on the side.

2. The kid wants free reign to choose any school based on the quality of the sports program, but the parents have financial constraints that may prevent pursuing the dream school.

3. The parents want their child at a big name school, but the kid has found a comfort zone with a coach and team at a lesser-known school.

4. The kid wants bragging rights of a top sports program, but the parents know that either the school or the sports program will be too much of a stretch.

5. The parents want their kid at the school that one or both of them went to, but the kid has no interest in walking in his or her parents' footsteps.

These mismatched agendas aren't insurmountable, but airing them will help drive which schools end up on your list and which you avoid.

Keep your sense of humor. Yes, college is extremely competitive as are college sports, but your child will end up somewhere, and even if s/he can't play a varsity sport in college, s/he can always play club or intramural. If you can keep your sense of humor throughout, it will help your child do the same.

And ultimately, try to find the right balance of taking control and letting go—the perennial parental dilemma. The lessons in parenting for you may be just as plentiful as the lessons in maturing and decision-making for your child.

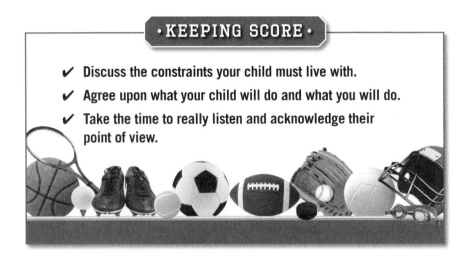

·KEEPING SCORE·

✔ Discuss the constraints your child must live with.

✔ Agree upon what your child will do and what you will do.

✔ Take the time to really listen and acknowledge their point of view.

CHAPTER 2

IS PURSUING A COLLEGE SPORT THE RIGHT DECISION?

Because you're reading this book, you've most likely decided that college athletics should be in your child's future. I'm going to offer you one last chance to revisit that decision. It's not for every kid and you should be sure that it's the right choice for yours. The high points are obvious. I would bet that if we all sat down and made lists of some things that are *appealing* about college sports, our lists would look pretty similar:

- ✧ Continuing to pursue a passion at a competitive level
- ✧ Enhancing the overall college experience
- ✧ Preparing for a professional career in sports
- ✧ Being part of a peer group that shares a common interest
- ✧ Possibly getting college paid for with an athletic scholarship
- ✧ Great fitness regimen
- ✧ And in our weakest moments—glory, fame, and bragging rights

But to really consider your child's best interests, you have to be aware of all the potential landmines buried beneath the path. The best case is that a sport will positively enhance your child's college experience and facilitate maturity in ways that might not have happened otherwise. But the worst case is that your kid will become disillusioned and frustrated, and the college experience may be compromised in ways you never anticipated. When I approached college coaches with the question of what kinds of unexpected challenges had the potential to derail freshmen student-athletes, there was no shortage of answers. Let me give you a sampling of the issues they came up with.

1. Time Management

Being a college athlete requires passing a crash course in time management. There are three areas of activity athletes will be involved in and must learn to balance:

- ⬦ **Academic commitments requiring class attendance and adequate study time**
- ⬦ **Time commitments for the sport including travel, practices, weight room sessions and workouts, games/matches, study halls, and so on**
- ⬦ **Social activities (need I say more?)**

While every college student has to learn how to balance academic and social activity, the student-athlete has to incorporate extraordinary incremental time commitments to pursue the sport.

You have to decide what is important to you and how you are going to manage your time. College sports require twenty hours per week per NCAA rules. There is not a lot of free time.

Pat Bailey, Assistant Coach, Baseball, Oregon State University

Playing at the D-I level is very time consuming. Off-season training, summer conditioning, study hall requirements, early morning practices, etc. take up a lot of time. I don't think most athletes going into it realize that their time is not their own.

Pat Kendrick, Head Coach, Women's Volleyball, George Mason University

D-I does not leave much time for college groups, internships, social organizations, hobbies, etc.

Catherine Wright-Eger, Head Coach, Women's Swimming, Purdue University

2. Athletic/Skill Parity

If you're considering college athletics, your kid was probably one of the best, if not the best kid on their high school team. Maybe they didn't even have to work very hard for that status, as the athlete who is naturally gifted may be able to coast through the high school years on their athletic talent alone. When they get to college, they are king of the hill no more. They are suddenly faced with a team full of kids who can justifiably lay claim to fanny space on that same throne. Not only do they no longer stand out, but now they must work harder than ever before just to keep pace.

First the kids need to realize that everyone playing, at any level, was a star in high school. Everyone was all-conference, all-state, or whatever. They are starting over from the bottom. It's like being in ninth grade all over. None of them were stars as freshman in high school and they shouldn't expect to be stars right away when they go to college.

Roc Bellantoni, Assistant Head Coach, Football, Eastern Illinois University

All are the star of their HS and Club teams. They have to learn to be psychologically strong within the environment and persevere when they aren't playing to their level and are running up the backs of teammates legs for playing time.

Diane Drake, Head Coach, Women's Soccer, George Mason University

Handling failure can be a big problem. A lot of kids have a tough time when they realize it is going to be difficult to compete at the next level. How they respond to the challenge, initially, often defines their collegiate experience. If they work hard and overcome initial failures or setbacks, they often come out better for the experience. If they look for excuses or just try to get by on the talent that got them there, they are unlikely to meet their goals and expectations.

Rob Miller, Head Coach, Men's Golf, Santa Clara University

Think hard about your kid's temperament and motivation. Some kids will be motivated to work hard and reach the next level, and others will be demoralized and not interested in putting forth the effort. Kids who just want to play but don't want to spend a lot of time working on their game to improve would probably be better off playing intramural sports where they can enjoy their sport and dominate without too much effort.

3. Managing Social Life

There are kids who are underachievers in academic pursuits and overachievers in social indulgences. College presents lots of temptations and the student-athlete has to be mature and responsible enough to keep them under control. Obviously, this includes partying, keeping late hours, and hanging out with questionable characters. Not as obviously, it also includes romantic relationships. Time expectations of a new boyfriend or girlfriend can be directly at odds with the time commitments of a student-athlete.

Once they get to campus, the biggest problem with the ones who struggle is that they do not attend the early morning class that most freshmen have. They sleep too much and stay up too late. The opportunity for social life is seven nights a week and some student-athletes can't say no to the temptations.

James Parady, Head Coach, Football, Marist College

Student-athletes often move from an environment in their home where routines are often set and guided by their parents and high school. In college, particularly a residential environment where I coach, students are forced from the first day to take much more responsibility in their daily lives with much less oversight. Students who have had problems have at times struggled with this freedom.

Joe Kinney, Head Coach, Baseball, Lafayette College

---

4. Physical and Athletic Requirements

Kids are often blindsided by the speed and physicality of the college game. Some will have the skills to stay competitive and others won't. There are also training regimens that are very demanding, particularly in D-I programs that have off-season practices and summer conditioning. D-III programs have restrictions on off-season training and practices but the players need to keep up on their own or they will fall behind. (See page 29 for a discussion of the various divisions.)

Athletically, the biggest challenges for incoming freshmen are adjusting to the speed and physicality of play and maintaining a consistent high level of performance.

Brad Stevens, Head Coach, Men's Basketball, Butler University

---

Some of the challenges are the level of play. Players are physically bigger, stronger, faster. Practice is longer but MUCH more intense than you ever had in your high school career...and there is pressure to perform on a daily basis.

Krista Kilburn-Steveskey, Head Coach, Women's Basketball, Hofstra University

---

The biggest problem we have with incoming student-athletes is that even though they are given a training program, most of them don't follow it and pick and choose what they want to do. Most will lift too much weight and not run enough to be in field shape when they come to camp.

James Parady, Head Coach, Football, Marist College

---

5. Parent Expectations/Over-involvement

Sorry. Time for some tough love. One issue some kids deal with is parent expectations that can't possibly be met. Perfect grades. First string starting spot. These are the baby boomer parents parading their "trophy kids." Give them a break. They don't have to be the best and the brightest to have a great experience, learn from it, and STILL become a fully functioning member of adult society. A second issue is parents who have always done so much for their kids that when they have to do it themselves, they're lost. Can s/he budget money? Get up on time? Do laundry? Make a decision? Stand up for what s/he believes in? If they haven't had the opportunity to do any of these things before college, let's just be thankful they will now have that chance.

All kids entering college have different maturity levels, which reflect their ability to take care of themselves. Before college, it's the parents who have managed the lives of many successful athletes. Some kids have done it on their own and there is everything in between.

Rob Miller, Head Coach, Men's Golf, Santa Clara University

Parents put too much pressure on kids to keep up grades and be first string. The kid can't make them happy. Another problem is the kids who were very sheltered. Need to teach them basics like how things work. Parents do too much of the heavy lifting.

Geoff Macdonald, Head Coach, Women's Tennis, Vanderbilt University

An unexpected challenge that can derail a D-I athlete is the lack of ability to make their own decisions and communicate with coaches due to helicopter parents.

Catherine Wright-Eger, Head Coach, Women's Swimming, Purdue University

Pages and pages of obstacles. The bottom line is that kids need to be so passionate about their sport that they are willing to forego much of what defines a typical college experience—sleeping late, hanging out with friends, socializing at night—in order to make the enormous time and energy commitment required to be a varsity athlete at the college level. And there are no guarantees that they will get the playing time that they are giving up so much for. If your child is not willing to make these sacrifices, college athletics may not be the right choice.

If anything you have read in this chapter makes you stop and reconsider whether your child is well-suited for college athletics, I feel a little bad, but, mostly, I feel like I helped point you in the right direction. The real message here is that we all go into the recruiting process with stars in our eyes and hope in our hearts. The reality is that college sports are probably tougher and more demanding than we could

THE INSIDE TRACK

College sports are much more demanding than high school or club sports, especially at the D-I scholarship level. Make sure you know what you're getting into.

ever have imagined. Now that you know that, are you still game? Okay then, let's figure out how to choose the right schools.

·KEEPING SCORE·

You should move ahead if you are fairly confident that your CHILD can:

✔ Balance the time management aspects of athletics and academics

✔ Accept teammates who are equally or more talented

✔ Resist the temptations of an overactive social life

✔ Handle the training regimen

And if you are fairly confident that YOU have:

✔ Managed your own expectations so you can accept less than perfection

✔ Adequately prepared your kid to handle day-to-day situations on his or her own

PART TWO

Creating Your College List and Finding the Right Fit

CHAPTER 3

ATHLETIC SKILL
ASSESSMENT

Many families have wasted a lot of time because of bad assumptions and pipe dreams about where their child can play. The athlete may have some inkling that s/he's not a strong candidate for Division I play but doesn't want to disappoint his or her parents, and s/he may not be ready to believe it either. Check your ego at the door; it's time to be honest about your child's place in the universe.

Waiting for the Call That Didn't Come

My friend's daughter Sarah spent a very successful four years playing basketball. As a senior she was clearly the player the team was built around. She figured she was good enough to play in college and that D-I coaches would come looking for her. It didn't happen. By the fall of her senior year, Sarah and her parents started to get a little panicky. They looked to Division III schools and found some interest. It was now very late in the recruiting game, and Sarah was lucky to find two schools that would still consider holding a spot for her. If she had realized earlier on that she was probably not a Division I player, she could have expanded that search to include far more than two schools. ■

Try to be as realistic as possible about where your child really fits. When you understand how competitive getting a college sports spot is, hopefully it will expand your thinking to consider a wider range of options, and you won't lose valuable time as a victim of inflated expectations. Sarah got tripped up for the same reason so many people get tripped up—her frame of reference for her talent was the small group of teams her high school played against. Your child may be the best or one of the best players on his or her high school team but it doesn't matter.

There are also college roster spots taken by international players that are not part of U.S. high school statistics. In 2004, there were approximately 18,435 high schools in the U.S. (National Center for Education Statistics: 2005). Here's the number of National Collegiate Athletic Association (NCAA) freshman roster spots available for a subset of NCAA sports:

NCAA Freshman Roster Positions Available (NCAA: 2/16/2007)					
Men's Basketball	Women's Basketball	Football	Baseball	Ice Hockey	Soccer
4735	4313	17501	8219	1135	5655

You do the math. The best player on every high school team may not be good enough to play in the NCAA **and that includes all three NCAA divisions**—never mind the full scholarship Division I level. In women's basketball, which was Sarah's sport, three out of four "best high school players" will not find a spot on a college basketball team. So rather than compare how good your kid is to the others on **their** high school team, what matters is how they stack up to the best players on **every other** high school team, and it's pretty tough for you to assess that. You also don't know how your high school program and the kids that play for it compare to other high schools. At a smaller high school with a program that is not as established, the best player on the basketball

THE INSIDE TRACK

Every high school team has a best player, a whole lot of high schools are out there, and there are a finite number of roster positions available to college freshmen.

team may not even be competitive with the sixth man on a team at a very big high school with a consistently winning record. And don't assume that if your kid plays club sports or Amateur Athletic Union (AAU) and is a strong player on that team that they're as good as any other club or AAU player. There is a wide range of skills on these teams, some tournaments attract tougher competition than others, and different parts of the country emphasize different sports. For example, a travel baseball player from the Midwest is not going to have the depth of experience that a travel baseball player from California, Texas or Florida has because of the weather differences that limit the Midwest to a shorter season than the warmer climates.

Matching your child's skill level with the right program requires an understanding of a variety of college-level athletic environments. Most of us are aware that there are three divisions in the NCAA—Division I, Division II, and Division III. Other options include the National Association of Intercollegiate Athletics (NAIA) and the National Junior College Athletic Association (NJCAA). Let me familiarize you with the differences between Division I, II, and III. You can get more info about the NCAA, NAIA, and NJCAA on their websites (ncaa.org, naia.org, njcaa.org).

NCAA Division I (about 333 schools as of 9/08)

If offered the chance, most kids would choose Division I for four very appealing reasons: scholarships, status, familiarity, and transition to the pros.

Scholarships—Division I offers full scholarships in several sports, covering the cost of college from soup to nuts. This makes college accessible and affordable, and these are awarded without any knowledge of the family financial situation, so you don't have to prove financial need to get one. Be aware that outside of basketball and football, many of the scholarships offered are partial, not full. But regardless of the amount, the offer of a scholarship dovetails nicely with reason #2.

Status—A scholarship tells the world that you're sought after and good enough at your sport for someone to pay your way. There is no underestimating the psychological value of this kind of public reinforcement for both you and your child. For you, it makes all those hours spent at games and tournaments, meets and practices, and camps and showcases worthwhile. Is status a good reason to choose a school? Sure. It may or may not be the *right* reason or the **best choice** for your child, but a little prestige may keep you warm at night. A Division I basketball player we know said that the best thing about becoming a Division I scholarship athlete is during your senior year in high school when everyone finds out about it. It's all about the bragging rights, baby!

Familiarity—These are the schools the kids know and the schools they've grown up following and dreaming about. They have favorites, and there is history and lore associated with them. These are the schools all their friends want to go to so they can sit in the stands and cheer "for their team." These are the teams they watch on television. Who wouldn't want it?

Transition to the pros—For kids who will make it to the professional level of their sport, the Division I scholarship provides the appropriate forum for the experience and exposure they need to be considered for the next level up—the pros. This is important for the rare breed elite athlete, but irrelevant for all but a few.

On Everyone's Radar Screen

Iman was the stud recruit every high school athlete dreams of being. He played AAU basketball with my son for a few years, and by the season after his junior year he was drawing huge crowds of coaches from top D-I basketball programs. Iman spent much of that summer attending the elite events sponsored by the major sporting goods manufacturers (you know who they are). The offers started pouring in. By the fall he had narrowed his list to seven, and then to three. His teammates loved to hear about his official visits because he was courted in a way few recruits will ever experience. We all remember the day he appeared on the TV sports channel, putting on the hat of the team he had finally chosen. He'll probably wear that uniform for a year or two, and then head for the NBA. A great story—and a rare one. These kids are few and far between. ■

NCAA Division II (about 294 schools as of 9/08)

Division II schools are less competitive than Division I, but Division II does have some scholarship money available. If your child is offered a chance to play at a Division II school, the school is more likely to offer a partial rather than a full scholarship, but a kid who needs financial help and doesn't have Division I offers will find Division II attractive for that reason. Most of the Division II schools would not be as recognizable to you by name as the Division I schools.

A Bird in the Hand

Denny really wanted to play Division I soccer, but he was never able to get attention from the D-I coaches. Financial aid was very important to his family, and a D-II school within two hundred miles of home came through with a partial athletic scholarship. Denny was an average student. His parents assumed that the offer he got from the D-II school would provide more assistance than any merit scholarship money he might get from a D-III school. Since the Division II offer was made in the fall, Denny needed to make his decision quickly or it would be extended to another candidate. Merit scholarship offers from D-III schools typically don't come until the spring of senior year. Since Denny didn't expect to get much given his academic credentials, he jumped on the D-II offer and attended that school. ■

NCAA Division III (about 444 schools as of 9/08)

Kids choose Division III because they either didn't have Division I options or their Division III options presented better fits. Jake's story at the end of this section is a good illustration of Division III presenting a better fit. A *BIG* difference between D-I and D-III is that *there are no athletic scholarships available at D-III schools*. Depending on the individual school, there will be need-based financial aid, and there may be (very generous) merit/academic scholarships, but full rides are few and far between. For many kids, the status of receiving *some* money for their academic abilities at a D-III school doesn't come close to measuring up to the status of receiving *a full ride* for their athletic abilities at a D-I school.

Other reasons kids choose D-III are because they're looking for a better athletic/academic balance, they want a smaller school, they want to be close to home, and/or they want to be an impact player and know that they will have a tougher time of it at the D-I or D-II level.

Because D-III is so large, there is tremendous variation in the skill level and time commitment required to participate, and there are some clear philosophical differences between programs within D-III as well. At one end of the spectrum are the schools that are more committed to academic pursuit, have minimal practice schedules and an overriding philosophy that college athletics are for fun and recreation. At the other end are the schools with sports programs that are more time intense and focused on winning while still educating their athletes—their teams could easily compete with D II or low major D-I teams. The only universal bond across the membership is the policy of not awarding athletic scholarships.

As you go through the recruiting process at the D-III level, be sure you understand and are comfortable with the philosophical leanings of the schools you're considering and the teams/conferences that will make up your child's day-to-day athletic life. These differences are reflected in comments from some of the D-III coaches in this chapter.

Not everyone is a standout Division I athlete. But remember that Division III can be just as intense as some Division I and II schools...it depends on the program.

Megan Eckenrode, Head Coach, Women's Field Hockey, York College

---

What level of basketball do they intend to pursue? They can spend valuable time trying to pursue unrealistic aspirations. If the student-athlete has received mixed reviews about his ability, then he and his family should proceed by pursuing various levels of basketball—and not just D-I, D-II, and D-III. There are sublevels in each division (top 25, top 100, top 200 programs nationally).

Andy Partee, Head Coach, Men's Basketball, Colorado College

Objectives Well-Defined Are Objectives Well-Met

Jake is the son of a friend and the oldest of four swimming siblings. He was a perfect D-III candidate. He was a better-than-average swimmer who loved to compete. But he didn't have record-breaking times, and he wasn't going to be recruited by a D-I program. Still, Jake wanted to continue swimming in college. His parents agreed, believing that discipline and physical exercise were both good for him. Jake had worked hard to overcome some learning difficulties and it was important that he be at a school where he could really focus on his academics and get extra attention if he started to struggle. There were several smaller D-III schools within a few hours of home that offered him a partial merit scholarship and a chance to swim on their team. He chose the one that had a student body that felt like the best fit for him and he's very happy there. ■

NAIA (about 284 schools)

Includes thirteen sports and about fifty thousand student-athletes. These tend to be smaller campuses and the schools are not as well known. More than 90 percent of NAIA schools offer athletic scholarships. The rules for inclusion in NAIA are less restrictive than the NCAA. For example, to be an NCAA member, the school must have at least one sport for each gender in each of three sport seasons (fall, winter, spring). NAIA schools are not subject to this requirement.

Junior College (about 503 two-year programs)

Why would a kid choose a junior college over a four-year school? As part of the college search process, you may want to consider a junior college if your child falls into any of these categories:

❖ **Your child's academic credentials need some work to qualify for an NCAA school at this point in time (see Academic Credentials in Chapter 5).**

❖ **Your child is not ready to leave home and would be better off living at home for a few years.**

- ✧ Your child is not enamored of the schools that are interested in him or her, and may be able to transfer to a more desirable school after two years in a junior college.
- ✧ You don't want the kind of financial burden the four-year college may entail—junior colleges are generally pretty inexpensive.
- ✧ Your child needs to work while attending school. Junior colleges will offer more evening and weekend classes that make normal working hours possible.

Temporarily Sidetracked

Josh was an ideal junior college candidate. He was a superb baseball pitcher during his freshman and sophomore years—one of the best in the area. But in his junior year he suffered a serious injury that took him out for the season, a critical period of time that coaches want to look at. Compounding Josh's situation were his academics. They just didn't meet the NCAA Clearinghouse Eligibility Center standards. Confident that his skill level wasn't permanently affected by his injury, Josh's goal was to get his grades and test scores where they needed to be to be eligible to compete in a D-I program. The best way for him to do this was to play at a junior college for a year or two and then transfer to a Division I school. ■

One or two years at a junior college may make student-athletes more desirable, either academically or athletically, and they will be able to transfer into a four-year college for the remainder of their eligibility. On the other hand, junior college may take them out of the mainstream and decrease their visibility to coaches of four-year programs, so it could work against them as well. Some junior colleges are going to do a better job of getting kids into four-year colleges than others. Ask the school for some statistics on how many kids were able to successfully transfer into four-year programs and continue playing their sport.

Prep School Option

Another option for athletes who either don't meet the NCAA Clearinghouse standards or are passed over for some reason is to put off college for a short time and attend a prep school after high school graduation. It won't affect their eligibility, and some prep school programs are designed to improve their academic standing and get them the exposure they might not have had. This can also be beneficial for the athlete who could use a little more time to develop physically.

Don't Forget to Have a Plan B

If you are still one of the people who believe that talented athletes will be found without marketing themselves, here's a story about a football player from a neighboring high school. Max was a 6'5" tall senior and weighed 265 pounds. He was a very talented player and a bright kid who just didn't get picked up. He decided to go to a prep school for an additional semester—not for the academics, but for the exposure for football players that the school is known for. Max got the results he wanted. He was offered a full scholarship to a strong Division I football program, started as a freshman, and became a freshman All American. How does a kid like that get overlooked? This shows once again that the system is not foolproof. And more important, that you can't assume that the coaches will come looking—even if your kid is D-I caliber. You have to do what you need to do to make sure they don't miss your kid. ■

MAKING THE SKILL ASSESSMENT

Now that you know a little more about the levels at which your child can play, how do you realistically assess their skill level, especially if they haven't played much outside of high school? Some of the ways you can assess skill level are listed on the following page.

- ✧ How much interest is coming from college coaches and from what kinds of programs
- ✧ Ask people who know the sport and are familiar with your child's skill level
- ✧ Participate in non-high school events and compare yourself to the competition
- ✧ Get statistics from your high school and AAU/club teams
- ✧ Consider your child's high school team experience
- ✧ Use the colleges' athletic websites to do research

Each one of the above is outlined more fully below.

How much interest is coming from college coaches and from what kinds of programs

If your kid was a serious Division I prospect, they would have probably been found already—Max is the exception, not the rule. Your zealousness will not turn a kid who doesn't have the skill into a college player, or a Division III player into a Division I elite major player.

THE INSIDE TRACK

Some kids will slip through the cracks and get found later in the process, but in all likelihood, your child will not be playing their sport at a big D-I school if they haven't been found by junior year.

Ask people who know the sport and are familiar with your child's skill level

Seek out the opinion of people who know your kid's skill level and who are around the sport. Make sure at least some of them have no financial stake in the outcome. Private trainers and AAU/club team coaches typically have a wealth of knowledge about both the sport and your child, but you need to make sure that their assessment is not being influenced by their desire to ensure your continued participation in their programs.

High school coaches, college coaches who have seen them play, and parents of upperclassmen teammates who have gone through the recruiting process in previous years are good sources with no financial stakes. Encourage them to be straight with you, but also try to understand what their rationale is for their point of view.

Participate in non-high school events and compare your child to the competition

If it is still early enough in the process, have your child participate in camps, showcases, and club teams. These give kids a good idea of how their skills stack up to others and help them determine where they might fit—making the process of narrowing down that much easier. If their only exposure is to their high school team and the conference it plays in, they just won't know how good they really are. When they start to play with and against kids from programs covering a broader area, they will get a much clearer sense of how far their skills will take them and what kinds of colleges to aim for. It may not be the news your child or you want to hear, but it will save you a lot of time and energy if you're not focusing your efforts on colleges where your child just isn't competitive enough to play.

Get statistics from your high school and AAU/club teams

Ask your child's high school coach or athletic director the following:

- ✧ How many varsity athletes playing the sport *at your school* have gone on to play at the D-I, D-II, and D-III levels in the past five years (and who are they)?
- ✧ How many varsity athletes playing the sport *in your conference* have gone on to play at the D-I, D-II, and D-III levels in the past five years (and who are they)?
- ✧ Then ask your child's AAU or club team coach the same questions.

Knowing how many have gone before will give you a pretty good idea of how competitive it is, and your child will probably know the players they mention—making it easier to gauge if and where s/he might fit based on a comparison to these players.

Consider your child's high school team experience

Use this very subjective rule of thumb: unless a serious injury intervenes, a future college player is probably starting on the varsity squad before senior year. In all likelihood, s/he is a starter no later than junior year, and should be recognized as one of the best players on the team as a junior. There may be boys who grow and mature late, and improve dramatically as seniors, but they are the exception, not the rule. Because girls physically mature earlier than boys, a future female college player could be expected to be a star on their high school team even earlier, as a sophomore.

Use the colleges' athletic websites to do research

There's also a lot you can learn about where your child will fit by looking at the athletic pages of schools' websites for your child's sport. Pick a few schools in D-I, D-II, and D-III and compare them.

> **Look at the backgrounds of the kids on the team roster. It will typically list their stats from their high school career and can provide you with a quick gut check on whether your kid's stats are or will be similar. If the majority of the roster were All State, All American, top scorers, etc., and your kid plays a more supporting role, that school is probably too much of a stretch.**

> **Look at the size and weight of the players. For some sports, the level at which your child can play will be more influenced by genetics than anything else.**

> **Look at the times for those sports where times are relevant (swimming, track). You will be able to determine if you fit in this roster pretty quickly.**

Finally, stay humble, recognizing how difficult it is to play a sport in college at any level. Based on the total number of freshmen roster positions available in NCAA schools at D-I, D-II, and D-III combined, the percent of high school seniors that will go on to play their sport in college looks like the following chart (source: NCAA.org):

Percentage of High School Senior Athletes Who Will Make a College Team	
Men's Basketball	3.0%
Women's Basketball	3.3%
Football	5.7%
Baseball	6.1%
Ice Hockey	11.0%
Soccer	5.5%

The percentages are probably a little higher when you include the NAIA schools and the NJCAA schools, but unless your child would consider going to a two-year school, the NJCAA is irrelevant here. So let's play this out. Assume your son or daughter plays basketball. Assume about fifteen or sixteen are on the high school varsity squad. Let's be generous and assume that eight of them are seniors. If only three out of one hundred will go on to play college ball, you would have to go through four high school teams to find one college player. See why it doesn't matter if your kid is the best one on their team? Also, you should now recognize that the difference between playing for a Division I school vs. a Division III school really amounts to determining if your child is in the top 1 to 2 percent or 3 to 5 percent (depending on sport) of high school seniors playing the sport.

Here's an example of how thinly sliced the top tiers are: a track coach at a D-I school told me that if you compare times in the 100M event, the difference between a scholarship kid and a non-scholarship walk-on/D-II/D-III kid is 3/4 of a second. That .75 seconds is marginally longer than the time it takes you to snap your fingers.

Stop the pity party if your child is not a Division I prospect, and take comfort in knowing that if s/he can play for an NCAA school at all, s/he has managed to beat out at least 94 percent of the high school seniors playing their sport. Use your instincts. Is your child in the top 1 to 2 percent of their sport? Then they very well may be a D-I prospect. If not, aim a little lower and know that the competition will still probably be much harder than what you expected.

What's the Downside of Making the Wrong Skill Assessment?

The typical mistake is that parents and student-athletes aim ***too high***. Again, because people use their local sports teams as their frame of reference, and because parents don't always see their children objectively, if their child is one of the better local players, they assume a D-I scholarship offer is in the future. When it doesn't come their way, those with unrealistic expectations are still willing to try to walk on and earn their spot. As one D-I lacrosse coach told me, "This is like putting them one floor higher on the elevator before they get pushed out of the building." If the kid has aimed too high, this can lead to disappointment down the line.

Parents and players are both stunned when they send their son or daughter (as walk-ons) to a level where they believe the sibling can play when, in reality, they do not have the athletic talent to play at that level.

Pat Bailey, Assistant Coach, Baseball, Oregon State University

---

If you aim only for D-I and it's a stretch for your child, two things can happen:

First, as several of the stories have already illustrated, kids may wait around to be found by a D-I program and it just doesn't materialize. With no backup plan to pursue their sport at a lower division, they will end up going to a college where they can't participate in varsity athletics, or they may get lucky, as Sarah did, and find a place to play at the eleventh hour. If Sarah had aimed herself correctly from the beginning, she could have explored many more schools than she ultimately did.

Second, kids can end up in programs that are beyond their skill level. Sometimes one good or lucky showing in front of the right person will do it. Sometimes an overzealous recommendation will do it. Initially, everyone is happy because it may involve a scholarship at a D-I or D-II school. However, if the program is beyond the skill level of the child, they won't play and will get increasingly frustrated when subsequent year recruits are still more skilled than they are and take the playing time they were hoping to earn over time.

Understand the level of play. One common misunderstanding is parents pushing their kids to a level too high. So many players end up either not playing or transferring out when they end up at too high a level.

Timothy Shea, Head Coach, Women's Basketball, Salem State College

Worse, if they're on scholarship, they can't quit the team or they'll forfeit the scholarship. Their options are to stick it out for four years, to transfer to another D-I school and lose a year of eligibility, or transfer to a D-III school where they may be able to play right away depending on how their skills fit with the team. If they transfer to a D-III school, they will have to forfeit their scholarship. Even under the best circumstances, transferring is an academic and social disruption.

Your goal is to start building a list of potential schools based on your assessment of which level or levels make the most sense for your kid: NCAA D-I, NCAA D-II, NCAA D-III, NAIA, junior college, or prep school. Note that at this point in time, more than one is appropriate.

· KEEPING SCORE ·

- ✔ **Figure out who you can ask to get an objective outside assessment and do it.**
- ✔ **Start your child competing in non-school events to gauge the competition outside of your community.**
- ✔ **Get statistics on recent recruiting history from your high school and club coaches.**
- ✔ **Do some initial website research by comparing the rosters of a sample of teams at all the different levels you're considering. This will also help you gauge where your kid falls.**

CHAPTER 4

PERCEIVED ROLE ON THE TEAM

Once a realistic skill assessment is made, the next dimension of fit will lead one student-athlete to one kind of school and another with the same exact skill level to another kind of school. Here is where personal needs and motivations come into play, and they will vary from kid to kid.

A Tale of Two Brothers

A Division III coach told me about two siblings who played soccer. Chris, the older brother, was in his program. His younger brother, Matt, played in the state tournament as a high school senior and because of the exposure was offered an eleventh-hour D-I scholarship. Matt spent his first year on the sidelines and it looked doubtful he would ever get much playing time. It just wasn't working for him. He transferred to the school where Chris was playing and is now making an impact in a successful and winning D-III program. Matt couldn't be happier. He learned the hard way that, for him, being a big fish in a small pond was better than being a minnow in the ocean of D-I. The coach summed up the impact of the transfer on this kid's overall college experience this way: When you're playing and the team is winning, the classes are easier, the food tastes better, and the girls are great looking. ■

This story speaks to understanding what motivates kids, and they don't always know until they're in the thick of it. Here was a kid who had a scholarship and could have been part of that program for four years, but he was unhappy because he wanted to play and was willing to give up his scholarship and D-I status to accomplish that.

At the core of his decision was the impact that he thought he would have in a Division III program vs. the lack of impact he was having in his Division I program. Every Division III coach can tell you stories about athletes they successfully recruited who had opportunities at both and chose the D-III option. The reason? They would rather play early and often in a very competitive D-III program that is likely to play into the postseason than be less of an impact player in a D-I program that rarely is competitive within their conference.

Another kid might choose the D-I option because of the prestige, the scholarship, or the quality and competitiveness of the program. Even if there are no guarantees that they will be able to play and have an impact, they just want to be part of that. It all goes back to understanding what wagon your child is most motivated to hitch their horse to. Here are two stories from kids that made the D-I choice instead:

Didn't Need the Spotlight

Mike was the star of the high school football team. His father played professional football, and it was assumed Mike would have his pick of schools. Mike was a good student and wanted to play in a big-time program at a strong academic school. But those coaches weren't calling. An Ivy League school heavily recruited him. Even though it met his academic standards, it wasn't competitive in the conference, and Ivy League schools don't offer athletic scholarships. Mike ended up a preferred walk-on at a Division-I school on the East Coast. No scholarship, but the right to earn a spot. He played on the practice squad as a freshman and on special teams the next year. He loves the school and being part of a big, successful D-I program. I asked Mike's parents if he ever considered playing at a D-III school, especially since he was not offered a D-I scholarship. They said no, Mike wanted to be part of a D-I program, even if it meant sacrificing playing time.

Sam had a similar story that was published in the *Chicago Tribune.* He was one of the\ best football players in the Chicago Public League but the scholarship offers just didn't materialize. Yale (D-I, but no scholarships) expressed interest, and the coaches assured him that getting in would be no problem. Sam learned a tough lesson about college recruiting when Yale turned him down in November of his senior year. In the midst of his panic, a tape of his just-completed senior season found its way to the running back coach at the University of Wisconsin. In February, he accepted a non-scholarship offer to play for the Badgers. This kid could have received merit-based aid to play at most any D-III school. But he made it clear that playing D-I ball was what he wanted most—even without a scholarship—when he said, "I want to play in the Big Ten, and Wisconsin is a dream come true. The opportunity to play at the highest level is worth not coming in as a top recruit." ▦

Some kids aim at a skill level that might be higher than their own because they are highly motivated by just having the chance to fight for a spot in a high-level program, or they are willing to be a practice player or bench warmer just to have the chance to be part of that kind of program. Other kids aim at a skill level where they can dominate or at least be very competitive because they are determined to be an impact player. Don't underestimate the importance of exploring these issues with your child at the beginning of the process so you can aim yourselves appropriately. *Just make sure it's your child's motivations driving this decision, and not yours.*

It may be your dream to see your child play in a particular conference or at a particular school, but if it's not your child's dream as well, pushing him or her in that direction may cause resentment and a less than satisfying college experience.

THE INSIDE TRACK

If it's really important to your kid that s/he's an impact player, don't aim too high or you will end up with one very disappointed benchwarmer.

First, you must have a realistic evaluation of yourself as an athlete and student. Many athletes/parents think they are D-I recruits. There are high- to low-level D-I programs. Some lower level D-I programs are competitively equal to high-level D-III. Be REALISTIC. Do you want to play? Do you want to be on the court or are you content to be a practice player at a higher level? Do you want a high-quality, perhaps expensive, education or do you want any college or university that will pay your tuition? Weigh all the factors. Are you accepting a scholarship at a school so that you can brag that you received a scholarship? Would you attend that school if you weren't offered the scholarship? What is your priority? Getting a basketball scholarship; getting an education from a school ranked in the top 25 nationally; getting the best education for the scholarship without playing time; getting the best education with tons of playing time and paying for it (D-I student-athlete going D-III)? It's all about the student/athlete and, more important, the student/athlete and parents being realistic.

Gerri Seidl, Head Coach, Women's Basketball, Carnegie Mellon University

Make a clear assessment of where you would fit into the team. Could you play at that level? Do you have the necessary skills and athleticism? Do you mind sitting on the bench for one to three years before you get considerable playing time? The more honest you are with yourself, the better choice you will make. And you should be picking the school on academics first.

Keri Sanchez, Head Coach, Women's Soccer, Claremont-Mudd-Scripps Athletics

In summary, make sure you go through the hard work of introspection and self-assessment. Mom and Dad, this means you too—not just your child. You have a lot invested in seeing your child through rose-colored glasses. The more you understand about your collective motives, needs, and your child's skills, the better positioned you will be to pick schools that are the right fit. Ask yourselves the hard questions and be honest and realistic about the answers.

·KEEPING SCORE·

✔ If your kid is more inclined to be an impact player, narrow your list by removing any schools that are a real skill level stretch.

✔ If your kid is more inclined to want to just be part of something bigger and better than they may be, narrow your list by removing any schools that wouldn't be enough of a challenge or wouldn't be enough of a competitive environment for them.

CHAPTER 5

ACADEMIC CREDENTIALS

How do your child's academic credentials figure into the college selection process? The easy answer is: the better their academic credentials, the more options they will have. ***Strong academic credentials will give them access to schools that kids who are better athletes but not as strong academically will not have access to, and will also give them access to merit-based scholarships at those schools.***

Student-athletes looking at D-I and D-II schools must meet NCAA Clearinghouse standards first, and beyond that, it's up to the school. Some will impose their own standards and some won't. If a player doesn't meet the clearinghouse standards, they will either need to spend a year at prep school or a junior college to try and get their grades up. If a player does meet these standards and the coach wants them, they're in. It's important to note that every school has its own internal standards and it's your job to ask the right questions to understand if your child can meet them. Meeting the NCAA Clearinghouse standards means that the schools are ***allowed*** to consider an athlete, not that they are ***obliged*** to. The schools in the Ivy League and Patriot League will have higher academic standards than the basic NCAA Clearinghouse standards, and so will schools like Northwestern, Duke, Stanford, UCLA, and UC Berkeley. Since the NCAA has clearly spelled these out, the process isn't open to fudging. But student-athletes who are looking at D-III schools must meet the academic standards of each specific school and will usually be held to the same standards that the general school population is held to. Let's look at the academic standards issue by division.

Meeting NCAA Clearinghouse Standards (for D-I and D-II only)

This is only relevant for NCAA sanctioned Division I and Division II schools, but in the early stages of your recruiting efforts, you won't know where your child will end up so it's probably prudent to go ahead and have your child register with the clearinghouse even if you're D-III focused. The clearinghouse partners with the NCAA to determine a student's eligibility for athletic participation in their first year of college enrollment. This is based on three criteria (accompanied by $50). The three criteria are academic record, ACT or SAT scores, and information about amateurism participation. Your child should initiate registration at the beginning of junior year and continue to send in relevant information throughout the year. Following are the basics of what you need to know. (Detailed information is available at www.NCAAclearinghouse.net, and questions can be answered at 877-262-1492.)

Academic Record/Test Scores

Meeting NCAA Clearinghouse standards requires completion of core courses in high school, and these differ somewhat for D-I and D-II. Note that the D-I list just got more rigorous, starting with students enrolling in college 8/01/08 and after. These minimum requirements will satisfy the clearinghouse, but any given school may have different and/or more stringent requirements. Check the academic requirements of any school you're seriously considering. Following are the clearinghouse requirements:

D-I: Must complete sixteen core courses

✧ Four years of English

✧ Three years of math (algebra 1 or higher)

✧ Two years of natural or physical science, including 1 year of lab science

✧ One extra year of English, math, or natural/physical science

✧ Two years of social science

✧ Four years of extra courses from the above categories, or foreign language, nondoctrinal religion, or philosophy

D-II: Must complete fourteen core courses

✧ Three years of English

✧ Two years of math (algebra 1 or higher)

✧ Two years of natural or physical science, including 1 year of lab science

✧ Two extra years of English, math, or natural/physical science

✧ Two years of social science

✧ Three years of extra courses from the above categories, or foreign language, nondoctrinal religion, or philosophy

D-I: The NCAA publishes a sliding scale of grades and test scores. They will compute your GPA based on your grades and add up the sums of the individual subtests within the ACT or SAT. You must meet both criteria. For example, if you have a 3.0 GPA, you must have a combined 620 on the SAT or a combined 52 on the ACT. If your GPA is 2.5, your SAT must be a combined 820 or ACT must be a combined 68. And if your GPA is 2.0, your SAT must be a combined 1010 and your ACT must be a combined 86. The ACT scores may not look like what you're used to because ACT scores are typically reported as individual subtest scores and a composite score, which is essentially an average of the subtests. The NCAA adds all the individual subtests together to arrive at their score. Go to www.NCAAstudent.org and download the most recent guide for the college-bound student-athlete. It's full of important information, including the sliding scale of grade point average and test scores for both ACT and SAT.

D-II: The calculation is a little simpler. You must have a 2.0 or better in your core courses and a combined SAT of 820 or a combined ACT of 68. There is no sliding scale.

Please note that the ACT or SAT scores must be reported directly from the testing agency. The clearinghouse will not accept scores reported on a high school transcript. When your child registers for the ACT, they can specify code "9999" to get their scores sent directly to the NCAA Clearinghouse. Alternatively, you can have them sent any time for an additional fee.

Amateurism Participation

Again, the criteria are slightly different for D-I and D-II, but this deals with issues like whether your child has a contract with a professional agent, has entered the draft to become a professional, has accepted salary or expenses reimbursement from a pro team, and has a contract with or is currently competing on a pro team. Have your child go to the website www.NCAAclearinghouse.net to start the registration process and everything will be spelled out.

D-III Academic Standards

While it is not necessary to satisfy the NCAA Clearinghouse standards, Division III is a little more complicated because every Division III school has its own academic criteria, and with few exceptions, your child will need to meet them. With 444 Division III schools to pick from, **the academic standards range from a willingness to take anyone with a pulse and a checkbook, to schools that are as selective as Ivy League schools**. Before your child gets his or her heart set on a D-III school based on the quality of its sports program, do a little snooping to make sure they are within striking distance of the academic criteria. Any of the standard guidebooks (Petersen's, Princeton Review, etc.) will provide statistics on the previous year's incoming freshmen, such as average GPA, percentage of kids who graduated in the top 10 percent and 50 percent of their class, and average ACT/SAT scores (technically, they usually report the score range of the middle 50 percent of students). You can also search the school's website for some basic statistics on the most recent incoming freshman class. Don't panic if your child doesn't meet every one of these criteria, but your gut will tell you if you're in the ballpark. The Prospective Students admissions link will tell you enough about the academic and test score credentials of the students at this school for you to know if your kid is within striking distance or if it's a pipe dream. Check to make sure they have programs of study in the academic area your child wants. If they're interested in studying molecular nanophysics, not every school will have a program of study available. Do this research before you contact a coach unnecessarily.

If your child has good academic credentials, and a strong academic program is a high priority, the good news is that you may actually be able to leverage the sport to gain admission to a more selective school than would have otherwise been available without the sport. The downside of this strategy is that you will be less likely to receive merit aid (see Chapter 8). Every school is looking for a range of students with unique ways of contributing to the student body. Athletic skill qualifies as a unique contribution and may give your child a leg up, particularly since every school needs to find students to fill its teams.

Leveraged His Way In

Scott was a cross-country runner who lived in a neighboring suburb. He always enjoyed running as a recreational activity, but didn't have a real love for it. He envisioned himself at a large public university and didn't see competitive running as part of his plan. Then, late in junior year, his times became very competitive, and his drive and passion ramped up. He decided he wanted to run in college, but at this point he was totally off the recruiting radar. Fortunately, cross-country running is a sport where performance can be measured, and Scott's parents e-mailed coaches a record of his times in different races. He got a number of positive responses and ended up at an Ivy League school. The coach there admitted that he tends to recruit runners locally, and that he never would have found Scott if he hadn't received the e-mail. Members of the Ivy League don't award athletic scholarships, but there is no doubt that Scott's talent as a cross-country runner helped distinguish him as an applicant at a very competitive school. ▪

Can College Coaches Help You Gain Admission?

The $64,000 question. First, understand that as a prospective recruit/ parent, a coach is obligated to tell you that admissions decisions are made in the admissions office, not in the athletic office. This is mostly true, but some coaches have more influence over the admissions decisions than others. The landscape looks like this:

- ✧ **Some coaches have no say in the admissions process at all, particularly in the most selective academic schools.**
- ✧ **Some coaches can indicate interest by submitting letters of recommendation or "top prospect lists" to the admissions office, but the final decision is still up to admissions.**
- ✧ **Some coaches have slots for "special admits" that they can use to get in just a few top prospects.**

Since you won't know which schools operate by which rules, you should ask. If a coach tells you that s/he can't guarantee your child admission, they mean it. Protect yourself by not putting all your eggs in one basket.

Parents think that coaches have more influence with admissions than they actually do. Contrary to what coaches might say, they often do not have a lot of pull with the admissions office.

Claus Wolter, Head Coach, Rowing, Franklin and Marshall

Coaches can assess the likelihood of admission by looking at the NCAA Clearinghouse status for D-I and D-II players. However, since D-III schools do not have to meet NCAA academic requirements, but will hold applicants to their own academic standards, a D-III coach will try to determine if your child has the minimum academic credentials to be considered. They will ask about your child's GPA and ACT or SAT scores. They may request an unofficial transcript. These are both good signs of interest. This will probably happen early on because they need to make a judgment about how likely your kid is to gain admission to the school. Especially in the current environment of burgeoning college applicants, rejections of students who seemingly fit the school's criteria are all too common, and the admissions office retains the right to accept or reject any student for any reason they want—there are no guarantees. At the most selective schools (those that accept less than a third of their applicants), don't assume that if your child falls in the middle 50 percent of GPA and ACT/SAT scores, that their acceptance is assured. These schools can and do reject many highly qualified applicants.

Let's be logical about this. It would not behoove the school to carry a roster full of sports teams with players that are all below the average academic standards of the school. It increases the chances that the athletes will struggle academically, and a roster full of failing athletes will keep coaches up at night. A few kids below the average can be offset by other team members that are average or above average relative to the rest of the school. Implication? A kid with stronger academic credentials (relative to the rest of the student body) is going to be more attractive to the coaching staff than the kid with identical skills whose academic credentials are weaker.

There are some schools that allow the coaches to have a few "special admits," which means that the coach can guarantee admission for a few student-athletes who meet some academic criteria known only to the coach and the admissions office. This is more the exception than the rule. In most D-III schools, the coaches either have absolutely no influence over the admissions process, or the coaching staff can give the admissions office a short list of prospects in priority order. However, even for the highest priority prospect, the admissions decision is still made by the admissions office and completely independently of the coaching staff.

At D-III schools, the vast majority of admissions decisions are made in the admissions office, not the athletic office.

Admissions is never a guarantee. Coaches have some pull and each university or college is different, but just because a coach goes to bat for a kid doesn't mean that they are going to be accepted.

John Browning, Head Coach, Men's Tennis, Emory University

In addition, the coaching staff is probably talking to four to six kids for each open spot, and some of those kids are going to want to come to the program and apply to the school even if they're not the coach's first or second choice for that position and not on their short prospect list. These applicants *will have to gain admission on their own merits.* Some of them will and some of them won't, depending on how they stack up relative to the full applicant pool for the school. This is why you hear stories about a kid who builds a relationship with a coach and is sure they'll get in, only to get a rejection letter from admissions in April. They feel blindsided, but it happens because *they just didn't realize they weren't one of the coach's top prospects, or even if they were, they couldn't get past the admissions requirements. D-III schools are about education first and the admissions office maintains control over most athletics admissions decisions.* Make sure you apply to some schools where you have the academic credentials to gain admissions.

Blindsided by the Admissions Office

Jon and Loren were the best senior players on their high school basketball teams. Both chose to apply to strong academic D-III schools. The coaches at these schools were very supportive, but since both kids were Regular Decision candidates (not Early Decision) they had to wait until April to get a final decision. Jon and Loren weren't worried because they had the support of the coaches and presumably the grades and test scores to gain admission. But these were and are challenging times to gain admission to schools with rigorous admissions standards, as the number of applications is astronomical. April came; acceptances didn't. Both were devastated. Loren quickly made a visit to a school she had applied to, and asked for a chance to be a walk-on. The coach liked her enough that she got a permanent spot on the team. Crisis averted. But in

Jon's case, he opted for a large state school and gave up the sport. He is probably more comfortable with his decision now, but it was a crushing blow at the time. ■

Impact of Division Choice on Graduation Rates

Based on a 1990 Federal law, the government now collects college graduation rates by school and aggregates that information by division. It can be found at www.NCAA.org. The following table looks at the percentage of incoming freshman from the fall of 2000 who went on to graduate within six years. It doesn't take into account walk-ons or athletes who transfer in, but it does include those who transfer out. The "all students" columns include everyone who attended, and the "student-athletes" columns include the student-athletes who were receiving athletic aid (i.e., at least a partial scholarship). Because Division III does not distribute athletic scholarships, there are no numbers in the "athlete" column for Division III.

FEDERAL GRADUATION RATES

Among freshmen who entered in fall of 2000, the percent who graduated by fall of 2006

Compiled in 2007 from NCAA Sources

	Student-Athletes			All Students		
	Men	**Women**	Total	**Men**	**Women**	Total
D-I	55%	71%	63%	59%	64%	62%
Men's sports:						
Basketball	46%					
Football	55%					
Baseball	45%					
Track	59%					
Other	61%					
Women's Sports:						
Basketball		64%				
Track		68%				
Other		73%				
D-II	48	64	55	43	51	47
D-III	N/A			60	67	64

There are two conclusions:

Your child is more likely to graduate if they attend a D-I or D-III school than if they attend a D-II school. This isn't a judgment about the quality of academics at one type of school versus another, but if completing an undergraduate degree is important to you and your child, it is more likely to happen at a D-I or D-III school.

Despite the time commitments and rigors of playing a sport in college, as a general rule student-athletes are just as likely to graduate as non-athletes. However, when you dig a little deeper, there are some differences:

Athletics appear to be *beneficial* for women—graduation rates were higher for women athletes in D-I and D-II schools than women in the general college population in D-I and D-II schools. For men, there were *mixed results*. Compared to the general male college population, athletes at D-I schools were less likely to graduate but athletes in D-II schools were more likely to graduate. (D-III was not included because there are no athletic scholarships.)

Men's basketball and baseball (D-I) are particularly vulnerable, with graduation rates almost 15 percent lower than men in the general college population.

If you're wondering whether or not your child's chances of completing their undergraduate degree will be compromised by playing a sport, this data suggests that for the most part, the answer is no. Will they have the same academic experience as someone who doesn't play a sport? Who knows, but they are just as likely to graduate.

· KEEPING SCORE ·

✔ Continue narrowing your list by excluding schools that your child doesn't have the academic credentials to gain admittance to.

✔ Include one or two stretch schools but make sure there are at least a few schools where they easily meet the criteria.

✔ Check that your child is on track to meet the NCAA Clearinghouse standards and start the registration process.

CHAPTER 6

ATHLETICS VS. ACADEMICS PRIORITY

Student-athletes have different agendas for the respective roles that athletics and academics should play in college. The personal agenda that you and your child share will guide which schools you end up targeting. *Think very hard about where you/your child fit on this continuum of athletic vs. academic priorities.* One is no better or worse than the other, you just need to determine what is right for you.

Athletic Priority

Some high school athletes care more about continuing their sport than their academics, and they will focus more on schools that have the best national reputation for that sport. Given a choice between a mediocre academic school with a strong sports team and a stronger academic school with a mediocre sports team, they are more likely to pick the former than the latter. If their motive for college is more about athletics than academics, priority will be given to schools that give them a full ride, regardless of the reputation or academic standards of the school. Kids who are either elite athletes or mediocre students are more likely to give athletics a higher priority.

Academic Priority

Other kids care as much or more about the quality of the education and the college experience they will have, and will only consider schools that can deliver on these criteria in addition to a positive sports experience. This may be an internal motivation and it may be driven more by their parents. They will try to get scholarship money if they can from a particular school, but they won't make their school choice based on money alone, and they won't attend a school that doesn't fit their non-athletic criteria just because they were offered money. Kids who are stronger academically and know they probably don't have a future in professional sports are more likely to make academics their priority.

The foundation of academic priority is set long before the college selection process. Let me give you a great example from my own experience. At a local AAU basketball tournament several years ago, a man sat next to me who had a son playing on the opposite team of my son's. He asked me which player my son was and then we went back to watching the game. When the game was over, he gave me his personal (and unsolicited) assessment of my son's strengths and weaknesses. Then he asked me what high school my son attended. After a minute of deep thought, he gave me his (again unsolicited) appraisal of the situation. He suggested that I should uproot my family, sell our home, and move to another school district that had a high school basketball program better suited to developing the areas he thought my son needed to work on. (Since these are all public high schools, you must live in the district to attend that school.) I mentioned that the school my son currently attended has a reputation for strong academics and that was part of the reason we chose to live in that community. The school he was suggesting did not. I couldn't imagine uprooting my family and switching my son to a lower quality academic environment for a basketball situation. He couldn't imagine passing up the opportunity to maximize a kid's basketball training in preparation for a basketball career. We clearly occupied opposite ends of the academic vs. athletic priority continuum.

When you're considering the role this plays on the colleges that will remain on your list, one main difference between D-I and D-III is that D-I programs tend to ***prioritize athletics over academics*** just by virtue of the time and travel commitment required.

Choose the school that meets your child's educational and emotional needs the best—not the school with the ten-time champions, free clothes, shoes, year-round competition and the like—remember, the bigger the sport and what goes with that, the less time for academics—and in the end, very, very few student-athletes will ever play their sport for a living.

Stuart Swink, Head Coach, Men's and Women's Tennis, Frostburg State

---

The choice of athletics over academics is also driven by the desire to get a scholarship and get at least some of it paid for. But scholarship aside, highly demanding athletic programs can take their toll on the student-athlete. In a *New York Times* article titled "Expectations Lose to Reality of Sports Scholarships," Bill Pennington wrote:

> *"Although those athletes who receive athletic aid are viewed as the ulti-mate winners, they typically find the demands on their time, minds and bodies in college even more taxing than the long journey to get there. There are 6 a.m. weight-lifting sessions, exhausting practices, team meet-ings, study halls, and long trips to games. Their varsity commitments often limit the courses they can take. Athletes also share a frustrating feeling of estrangement from the rest of the student body, which views them as the privileged ones. In this setting, it is not uncommon for first- and second-year athletes to relinquish their scholarships."*

D-III programs aim for more of an ***academic/athletic balance***. Un-doubtedly, you can get a great education at a D-I school if you're an athlete, but the demands of the sports program will make it that much more chal-lenging. The Division III schools attempt to maximize all three parts of the "triangle," which are the student's academic, athletic, and social experience at college. Remember Jake, the swimmer? Even if Jake had been a D-I caliber swimmer, he may have still chosen a D-III school to ensure that he would have the time to focus on his academics, particularly given his history with learning challenges.

The Division III philosophy is academic-based with a secondary focus on athletics. This does not mean that we as coaches do not take the athletics seriously. The 'athletic' part of things are the coaches focus, but we do understand that academics is also a very high priority.

Aaron Olswanger, Head Coach, Men's and Women's Cross Country, University of Redlands

The most highly selective Division III schools have the reputation of being prestigious academically, yet still presenting the college athlete with a good balance between academics and athletics. Even in a very fine Division I academic school such as those in the Ivy League or Patriot League, the time commitment a sport entails at this level may undermine your child's academic experience or, for that matter, your child's overall college experience. ***So how do you know just how demanding any given sports program is?*** This is a tough question to answer because there's no comparative measure, and even within D-III, some programs will be much more demanding than others. Your best tactic is to ask the coach and the other players. Here is a series of questions to consider asking:

For the coaching staff:
- How much time is devoted to/what is the schedule for practices?
- How much time is devoted to/what is the schedule for weight training?
- When are the competitions typically scheduled/how often do the students miss class?
- How much travel time is involved?
- What is the off-season training/workout expectation?
- How many credits is it reasonable for players to take per semester?
- In the past few years, how many players have dropped out of the program because it was too demanding of them?
- What are the graduation rates of players in the program in the past few years—what percent of the players graduate in four years?

And here's one that forces the coach to make a comparative assessment:

✧ If you had to compare the demands of your program to the demands of other programs in the same conference or division, would you say your program is more demanding, about the same, or less demanding. If it's more demanding, in what way?

For the other players:

✧ Have you had any problems balancing your schoolwork and team commitments? If so, what kind of problems, how did you solve them, and how much support did you get from the coaching staff?

✧ How often do you have to miss class and how do the faculty react to that?

✧ Does the team commitment take more time, about the same amount, or less time than you expected?

Brother Knows Best

Sometimes kids learn from each other, especially if they have an older sibling who has survived the college recruiting process. In a family of three very athletic boys, the oldest son was a D-I athlete at a prestigious East Coast school. The middle son accepted a full athletic scholarship to play football at a large state university in the Midwest where he learned quickly that playing football at that level leaves no time for academics or a social life. Also that winters there were really cold. Along came the third son—the strongest student of the three. He was a big kid and a talented football player, but after talking with his brother, he knew that D-I football wasn't for him. He was looking for strong academics and a smaller school. He chose an academically oriented D-III school from among the many recruiting him who were anxious to add a 250-pound player with a 32 ACT to their offensive line. ▪

· KEEPING SCORE ·

✔ If the highest priority is *athletic*, keep your list as is, because so far it has been constructed around your child's athletic skills and the role they want to play on their team.

✔ If the highest priority is *academic*, trim your list based on the kinds of programs that will let you focus in that way.

CHAPTER 7

NON-ATHLETIC COLLEGE PRIORITIES

This chapter includes all of the things that may be important to kids but aren't directly related to their sport. There are many considerations that can result in your child feeling like a great fit *or* a misfit. Following are some of the general school criteria that may be important to your child.

Size: Large vs. medium vs. small

This refers not only to the size of the overall student population and the campus, but also to the size of the classes. Some kids are happy to hide in the back of a class of two hundred and some do much better in a smaller class with more individual attention. Large schools will generally have larger classes with less personal interaction than smaller schools, but they may have a broader range of classes to choose from.

Setting: Urban vs. suburban vs. rural

Will your child be happy if the campus is his or her whole social life or does s/he need access to a city and a little more action to be happy?

Campus life

Some schools have a bustling campus and are the hub of activity for the community. This is often true of schools in smaller towns that don't have access to a city. Other schools, particularly those in the middle of a big city, have less participation in campus life because there are so many other options available. Similarly, some schools have a large percentage of students living on or near the campus so there's always action, while other schools have a much bigger commuter population and the campus becomes a ghost town on the weekends.

A Case of Tunnel Vision

Brian was a lacrosse player from the Midwest who wanted more than anything to play college lacrosse. The only coach that expressed serious interest in him was from a small D-III school in Pennsylvania. Brian admitted he decided to go there to play lacrosse, not because he was sure it was the right place for him. Frankly, besides the team statistics, he didn't know that much about it. He soon realized that the college was primarily a commuter school and that the campus was awfully lonely on the weekends. This was information he could have discovered in any college guidebook. Even though he was a starting attack-man on a winning team, he was not happy. He finished his freshman year and moved home to take some time off and figure out where he wanted to continue his education. Brian knows that he has to look beyond the lacrosse field before he makes his next move. ▨

Proximity to home

This is a deal breaker for lots of kids, and parents as well. Is it important that your child is within driving distance of home or is it okay if s/he has to fly home for visits? As parents, are you planning on attending many of your child's games/matches, and if so, are there distance limitations for you? This may be important if you are used to watching your kid compete.

Weather

Not everyone loves the snow, not everyone loves humidity. If you have a kid who has grown up in warm weather and shudders at the thought of snow, or if you live in a cold climate and your kid hates the humidity, take that into consideration. For kids who love the change of seasons, a year-round temperate climate may not cut it.

College has curriculum for chosen program of study

If a school doesn't have a program for what your child wants to study, it can present a big problem. This should be one of the first things you check when you're researching the schools. Even if the school has your child's expected course of study, find out if the athletic department puts any limitations on the courses or major s/he intends to pursue. On the other hand, many kids go into college not knowing what they want to study and change majors three times before it's all over. If your child is undecided, then this isn't as important.

Public vs. private

This criteria may have big dollar implications because private schools tend to be much more expensive but may provide more financial aid.

Religious affiliation

Is this important? If so, know the religious affiliation of the school and how it impacts campus life.

Extensive sports program to experience as a spectator

Some kids really want to be at a school where they can major in being a fan for four years. How important is observing big-time sports (for the sports your child isn't participating in)?

My son couldn't imagine college without a ball in his hands. He was willing to compromise almost anything as long as he could play in what he considered a competitive program. One of his best friends played football but wasn't a Division I prospect and was willing to give it up to get the bigger rah-rah college experience that a larger Division I school would offer him as a spectator. He applied to one smaller school where he would probably be able to play football, but most of his applications went to larger Division I schools where he would be watching from the stands. That's where he ended up and he has no regrets.

Availability of financial aid

Don't fret—that section is coming next.

School culture

Is it a good mix or is it more homogeneous? Are the majority of kids clean-cut, preppy, bohemian, conservative, partiers, studiers, etc. Feeling like they fit in with the kids on campus is one of the most important criteria for a lot of kids.

Study abroad programs

THE INSIDE TRACK

Committed student-athletes may overlook the non-athletic characteristics during the recruiting process when sport is king and campus life is still a distant abstraction. But once they're at school, if they've made bad choices about the non-athletic attributes that are important to them, they will regret it.

Does the school offer one that your child is interested in? If s/he participates in athletics, can s/he still participate in the study abroad program? Some schools may offer summer options that are accessible to athletes, others won't.

Greek culture

How important are fraternities and sororities? Would your child rather be somewhere that does or doesn't have a large Greek scene?

Non-varsity sports

Does the school offer club or intramural sports? There may be sports other than the varsity sport your athlete competes in that s/he wants to play more recreationally. If s/he ends up not being recruited to play his or her sport at a varsity level, it may be important that s/he can play on a club or intramural team.

Make sure you look at the school as a whole, beyond just the athletic department. Yes, athletics will be a big part of your college career, but you need to find a school that meets your academic needs and is the type of community you will enjoy and thrive in. I always tell recruits: You must find the schools that fit, then explore athletics.

Sarah Davis, Head Coach, Volleyball, College of Wooster

·KEEPING SCORE·

✔ List any non-athletic priorities that will be a deal breaker if they aren't met.

✔ Narrow your list based on these priorities.

✔ Make sure you and your child agree on this list because you won't necessarily have the same priorities to start.

CHAPTER 8

MONEY CONCERNS

Now it's time to take a look at the elephant sitting in the middle of the room. There is no bigger issue for most parents than how to get their kid's college education paid for, and ***there is probably no area more misunderstood than how scholarships work in the different divisions***. The bad news is that, yes, college costs a lot, but the good news is that there is a lot of money available if you know where to look—and it's not necessarily where you expect to find it. Let's start with the money that everyone knows about: the athletic scholarship.

What are your kid's chances of getting a scholarship?

Don't count on it. I'll use NCAA basketball as a sobering example. Division I schools are limited by the NCAA to 13 men's and 15 women's basketball scholarships and Division II schools are limited to 10. Division III schools don't give athletic scholarships. Using men for the example, 333 D-I schools yields 4329 scholarships, and 294 D-II schools yields 2910 scholarships. That's a total of 7239 scholarships across the divisions. Let's assume that a quarter of the team will be incoming freshman. That results in a total of 1809 available scholarships, which doesn't sound

THE INSIDE TRACK

Your child's chance of getting a scholarship is only slightly better than one in one hundred.

so bad until you consider that there are 157,000 high school basketball-playing seniors.

Many parents make the blanket assumption that Division I and Division II schools offer scholarships and Division III schools don't. In reality, parts of this are untrue, and it is generally too simplistic a characterization. Whether your child is offered a full or partial athletic scholarship will depend not only on division, but on school and sport as well, and while Division III schools don't offer athletic scholarships, many of them have plenty of money to share.

In Division I and Division II

Here are some basics about how Division I and Division II scholarships work in the NCAA. First, scholarships are for one year only and are renewable each year. There are no four-year scholarships—the NCAA prohibits them. The obvious implication is that if there are serious problems with a particular athlete, the school can choose not to renew a scholarship, and every year there are a number of kids on athletic scholarships at D-I schools that have their scholarships revoked for a variety of reasons. There are many circumstances that might result in a scholarship not being renewed. For example, there may be a head coaching change and the new coach may "clean house" to make room for his or her own players. While this can't be avoided or even anticipated, before accepting a D-I scholarship, a prospective athlete should evaluate the stability of the coaching situation and the direction that program is moving (up, down, or stagnant). A program in trouble may have a coaching change on the horizon. Another example is when a coach decides that a specific student-athlete isn't good enough to play at that level, or isn't as good as someone else they need the scholarship for. Harsh? Yes, but coaches are hired and fired on the basis of a teams' success, and a player who can't contribute what's expected becomes a liability.

For each sport, there are a maximum number of scholarships allowed. This doesn't mean that each school *must* offer this many scholarships; it means that by NCAA rule a school is *limited* to that many. Schools may choose to offer fewer, none, or not offer the sport at all. The allotment is generally less for Division II schools than Division I schools, which is one of the reasons why it is harder to get a full ride in a Division II school. Following are the allotments by sport:

NCAA-Allowed Scholarship Allotment
(Maximum number of full scholarships allowed in an academic year)

	Men		Women	
	Division I	Division II	Division I	Division II
Archery	n/a	n/a	5	9
Badminton	n/a	n/a	6	10
Baseball	11.7	9	n/a	n/a
Basketball	13	10	15	10
Bowling	n/a	n/a	5	5
Cross Country Track & Field	12.6	12.6	18	12.6
Equestrian	n/a	n/a	15	15
Fencing	4.5	4.5	5.0	4.5
Field Hockey	n/a	n/a	12	6.3
Football		36	n/a	n/a
Bowl Subdivision	85		n/a	n/a
Champion Subdivision	63		n/a	n/a
Golf	4.5	3.6	6	5.4
Gymnastics	6.3	5.4	12	6
Ice Hockey	18	13.5	18	18
Lacrosse	12.6	10.8	12	9.9
Rowing	n/a	n/a	20	20
Rifle	3.6	3.6	n/a	n/a
Rugby	n/a	n/a	12	12
Skiing	6.3	6.3	7.0	6.3
Soccer	9.9	9.0	14.0	9.9
Softball	n/a	n/a	12	7.2
Squash	n/a	n/a	12	9
Swimming/Diving	9.9	8.1	14	8.1
Synchronized Swim	n/a	n/a	5.0	5.0
Team Handball	n/a	n/a	10	12
Tennis	4.5	4.5	8.0	6.0
Volleyball	4.5	4.5	12	8
Water Polo	4.5	4.5	8	8
Wrestling	9.9	9.0	n/a	n/a

You may be wondering why some of the figures in the preceding chart are not whole numbers. There are two different designations: ***equivalency sports*** and ***headcount sports***. For a ***headcount sport***, each athlete on scholarship counts toward the maximum headcount the school can have on scholarship, so whether a player is given a full athletic scholarship or given only one dollar, s/he is counted toward the headcount for that sport. Since a men's basketball team can only have thirteen scholarship athletes in their headcount, a school might as well offer thirteen full scholarships so it can attract the thirteen best players possible. For headcount sports, full scholarships are more common. The list is not long. Men's headcount sports are basketball and football, and women's headcount sports are basketball, gymnastics, tennis, and volleyball.

For an ***equivalency sport***, coaches have a certain total dollar amount in the "scholarship pot," but can split it up among multiple athletes in any proportions they want. They can carry more athletes on partial scholarships and this provides the opportunity to develop more players. It is harder to get a full scholarship in an equivalency sport because it is in the coach's best interest to use the allotment of scholarship money to get as many high-potential athletes on the team as possible. Every other sport offered at the collegiate level not mentioned above as a headcount sport is an equivalency sport. Look back at the chart for a minute. You will notice that D-I men's soccer allows 9.9 scholarships and D-I men's volleyball allows 4.5. With eleven soccer players on the field at a time, and six volleyball players on a court, even all of the first string players can't be awarded full scholarships. And don't forget all the other players waiting on the sidelines. For most sports, partial-scholarship athletes, walk-ons, and non-scholarship athletes are an important part of the mix.

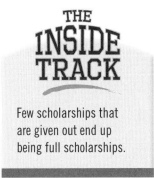

Few scholarships that are given out end up being full scholarships.

Bill Pennington comments on scholarships in his previously mentioned *New York Times* article:

> *"Excluding the glamour sports of football and basketball, the average NCAA athletic scholarship is nowhere near a full ride, amounting to $8,707. In sports like baseball or track and field, the number is routinely*

as low as $2,000. Even when football and basketball are included, the average is $10,409."

Interestingly, in the sports where both men and women compete, women tend to get higher value scholarships, probably to balance the disproportionate amount of scholarship money awarded to men for football. Considering how difficult it is to get an athletic scholarship, coupled with the likelihood that it will only cover a limited amount of your child's overall college expenses, ***the smart course of action is not to count on a scholarship and have a backup plan for getting your child's education financed***.

In Division III

Now, let me address the myth that Division III schools offer no financial support to student-athletes. Many of the coaches I surveyed when researching this book told me that ***there are more misunderstandings about financial aid than anything else*** and they run the gamut. As one example, some parents don't know that D-III programs are forbidden to give ***athletic*** scholarships. When a coach tells them he can't help out financially, they assume the coach is holding out for someone else. Honestly, s/he isn't. When I asked coaches about the most common misunderstandings between them and student-athletes and their families, this was the mother lode.

Parents think if they really want your kid, they will get him admitted and get him a good aid package. Not true! A lot of schools cannot control the admissions process, and the NCAA does not allow us to be involved in the financial aid process.

Richard Lackner, Head Coach, Football, Carnegie Mellon University

---

Other families assume that if there is no athletic scholarship money, they must pay full price, and they don't realize how much money is actually accessible—it's just not "athletic" money. While it is true that Division III schools are forbidden by NCAA rules to award ***athletic*** scholarships, there is money available for families that can show ***financial need***, and the individual schools can award scholarship money based on ***merit, academic performance, community service***, or anything else the school deems appropriate.

A big misconception about small Division III schools is that they are too expensive and, with no athletic scholarships, impossible to afford. But if a student coming out of high school has high grades, good ACT/SAT scores, and good class rank, s/he can be eligible for many scholarships that cover two-thirds of the tuition at many D-III institutions. With other grants, the costs can sometimes be cheaper than going to the large D-I schools.

James Akita, Head Coach, Men's Track and Field and Cross Country, Elmhurst College

How many talented kids who would be perfect fits for D-III athletics never pursue them because they don't think they can afford it? You should consider any and all schools that look like they would be a good fit and let them tell you what their best financial offer is before you assume it won't be good enough. And please reinforce to your child how important grades and test scores are in high school.

If your kid loves his or her sport but just isn't as athletically gifted as some others, this is one way to broaden their options and eliminate a lot of competition. And there is money.

THE INSIDE TRACK

Strong academic credentials will give kids access to schools and merit-based scholarships that others who are better athletes, but not as strong academically, will not have access to.

Where There's a Will, There's a Way

My nephew Dustin played high school football and was captain of the varsity team his senior year. As an All-American with a decent academic record, he was hoping to play at Texas A&M or Penn State. He sent his information and videotape, but it was a case of unrequited love with genetics to blame. He was just too small to play in a D-I program. He turned his sights to a D-III school an hour from home. Dustin's dad was between jobs at the time, and was concerned that a D-III school meant no scholarship money. But Dustin was able to qualify for need-based aid. He also received a $3,000 merit scholarship and borrowed a few thousand dollars annually on a low-interest government-backed loan. The upshot was that despite a $25,000 price tag, the family paid only $8,000 the first year. Then Dustin's dad landed a good job and the need-based aid came to an end. The family considered looking for a less expensive option, but by then Dustin was so committed to his school, team, and coach that they made it work. He graduated with a marketing degree and has been very successful. Did his parents spend more than they planned to on their son's education? Yes. But do they have any regrets? None.

And here's an interesting twist to the story. Dustin's younger sister, Megan, started at the same college her brother's senior year. Her grades and test scores were better, and she was awarded a Presidential Scholarship (a fancy term for a merit scholarship) of $12,000 a year for all four years. Megan's education ended up costing a lot less than Dustin's because of her academic credentials. But for those of you keeping score, her parents point out that their daughter is getting married shortly and the cost of her wedding will easily even the score. ▪

This story illustrates several important points:

First, if you're concerned that your finances won't allow you to afford a D-III school without an athletic scholarship, the exact opposite may be true—the less financially able you are, the more need-based aid you will probably qualify for. See what they'll offer before you take the school off your list of considered schools.

Second, see the impact of good academic credentials? Megan was not an athlete, but her strong academic credentials quickly earned her half of her total yearly costs before the family applied for any need-based aid or any additional scholarship money.

Third, Dustin leveraged his great college experience into a successful start in the working world, and isn't that the point of a good education in the first place? Undoubtedly, his perseverance as a four-year college football player and varsity captain helped employers look upon him more favorably when he was job hunting.

A $500 Question

So now you see how tough it is to get a large athletic scholarship. Suppose someone gave you five hundred dollars to invest toward your child's athletic future. How would you spend it? You may be inclined to hire a personal trainer, or suggest s/he join a gym or club team, in the hope that your child's skills will improve and better position him or her for a scholarship. I am going to show you that a better use of that money would be to invest it in a tutor or ACT/SAT prep course. It might not be as much fun for your kid, but you will definitely have access to more scholarship money by improving grades and test scores than by improving athletic skills. Here's some proof. The table below shows the percentage of full-time undergraduates at four-year institutions that received institutional merit-based grants; that is, money that was awarded by the school (not the government) for merit (not need). It is presented by college grade point average (GPA). What it shows is that *the higher the student's GPA, the more likely they were to get merit aid*. Also, money was awarded to a much higher percentage of students at private schools than public schools, so don't be scared off by the initial sticker shock of the costs at a smaller, private school. They may come through for you with substantial aid, particularly if your child has good grades and test scores.

Percentage of Full-Time Undergraduates at Four-Year Schools That Received Institutional Merit-Based Grants: 1999–2000		
College GPA	**Public School**	**Private School**
Less than 2.0	5.1	19.4
2.0–3.5	7.5	27.2
3.5 or more	20.3	39.3
(Source: U.S. Dept. of Education NCES, 1999–2000 National Postsecondary Student Aid Studies)		

Okay, so it makes sense that more merit money would be awarded to kids with better grades. *But the more shocking comparison is the money awarded for academic skills vs. the money awarded for athletic skills.* Let's compare the amount of money that is available through merit scholarships based on academic criteria, with the money that is available through athletic scholarships at the D-I and D-II levels. Since all athletic money is awarded from the specific schools, this represents the total sum of athletic money awarded from four-year institutions. The merit figure represents only that money which is awarded through the specific schools and doesn't include federal or state grants, so it's a very conservative estimate. Also, the merit scholarship info is based on 2000 data and the athletic scholarship info is based on 2004 data, so the actual difference would probably be greater than what I'm showing here if more recent merit scholarship data were available.

Total Scholarship Dollars at Four-Year Colleges Distributed for:	
Athletics*	Academic Merit**
1.7 billion	7.7 billion
*(*Compiled from NCAA Sources, 2004, and NAIA, 2004)* *(**U.S. Dept. of Education NCES, 1999-2000 National Postsecondary Student Aid Studies, and U.S. Census Bureau, 2000 Census)*	

D-III Schools Are Not Equally Generous

D-III schools vary on the amount of merit-based financial aid they have to give, so make sure you understand the scholarship and financial aid options at each school you're seriously consider-ing. If you can find out about the endowment the school has, this will give you an indication of how much there is to go around. There are exorbitant numbers of applicants to all colleges these days, partly based on demographic trends (all of the babies of those baby boomers coming of college age), and partly based on how easy it is to apply to multiple schools when so many of the Division III schools use the Common Application form. As a result, applications are up and, therefore, schools must be more selective and must reject more kids. ***One by-product is that the more selective the school is, the less likely it may be to offer merit (or any other non-athletic) money.*** Among the

THE INSIDE TRACK

Merit dollars outnumber athletic dollars more than four to one. So which is the better investment?

schools my son looked at, those that accepted no more than one-third of the applicants were stingy with offers of non-athletic scholarship money. The schools that accepted more than a third were more generous.

At a small, private, liberal arts school on the East Coast, the coach told an interesting story. He was entering his fourth year at this school. During his first year, 40 percent of all students who applied were accepted and merit scholarships were available for team members who "qualified." Three years later, only 28 percent of the applicants were accepted and no longer were there any merit scholarships being awarded. Of course, in that time, the cost of attending this college had also gone up, making the sticker-price shock even worse. The enrollment was kept at the same level, so many more kids were applying, and with long lines waiting to get in, the school wasn't as reliant on dangling scholarships to entice students to attend.

How Do You Compare Schools on Merit Money Awarded?

There is information available to help you figure out who's giving what so you can target the schools that are more likely to give you merit money, or are less expensive to start with. Some of the mainstream college guides provide this information. The best source I found was *Peterson's Four-Year Colleges* (updated annually). For each school listed, this guidebook provides the following financial aid facts:

- ✧ **Number of applicants judged to have need and number who had their need fully met**
- ✧ **Number of non-need-based (merit) awards given and average amount of money**
- ✧ **Average percentage of need met**
- ✧ **Average financial aid package**
- ✧ **Average indebtedness upon graduation**

Before you completely glaze over, let me give you an example of three D-III schools. The variations in cost, selectivity, and their approach to financial aid show there is probably a school for everyone. Williams College in Massachusetts is an exclusive liberal arts school, Illinois Wesleyan is a somewhat selective liberal arts school in Illinois, and Frostburg State is a less selective public school in Maryland. Here's a comparison of the three based on data available in the Peterson guide:

	Williams College	Illinois Wesleyan	Frostburg State
Undergraduate enrollment	2017	2146	4321
Percentage of applicants admitted	19%	57%	76%
Approximate costs	$40,310*	$35,790**	$13,058***
Number judged to have financial need	812	1164	2033
Percent to have need fully met	100%	56%	26%
Number receiving non-need-based awards	0	668	438
Avg. $ amount of non-need-based award	-	$8,691	$2,452
Average debt upon graduation	$10,753	$21,846	$15,678

*2005-06 school year
**2006-07 school year
***In-state for 2006-2007 school year, almost 90 percent of students are in-state

These are all D-III schools with under five thousand students but with very different approaches to financial aid.

Williams College is highly selective and chooses to fully fund anyone who has financial need, but gives no merit-based aid. This allows them to continue to attract the best and brightest regardless of their ability to pay, and because they are so selective, there is always a waiting list of students willing to pay their own way so Williams can get away with not giving merit money. Even though this is the most expensive school of the three, students leave with the least amount of debt because those who were most in need had all of their need met.

Illinois Wesleyan only partially funds financial need, but is very generous with merit-based aid, awarding merit aid to almost one-third of the student population. Keep in mind that this aid is awarded without regard to a family's financial situation. This school attracts better students by enticing them with merit aid.

Frostburg State is much less expensive to start with (as long as you're an in-state student) and is not as generous with either need-based aid or merit aid, but doesn't have to be because costs are lower.

In addition to Division III schools, Ivy League schools (Division I) do not give athletic scholarships. Similar to Williams College, the Ivy League awards need-based scholarships but no merit-based scholarships. In other words, if you can't establish financial need at these schools, you will be writing big checks every year. But there is some hopeful news. A recent trend that started at Harvard and is trickling down to other schools is a greater use of their endowment to fund students in need. As of early 2008, Harvard's policy is to fully fund the education of any student they accept whose family income is $60,000 per year or less, and for families making between $120,000 and $180,000, they will only be asked to contribute 10 percent of their income. Since acceptance decisions are made without any knowledge of a family's financial situation, there is no discrimination against students who will require more financial aid to attend. Other prestigious schools (Yale, University of Pennsylvania, Pomona College, Swarthmore College, and Haverford College) all announced they would eliminate loans—essentially replacing loans (which must be paid back) with grants (which do not need to be paid back).

What Else Can You Do to Get Money from a D-III School?

Other than need-based financial aid, you should now recognize that D-III schools are more generous with scholarship money for strong academic credentials (merit money) because that is what makes an applicant most attractive to them, and any other skills they bring also help to round out the college community. Focusing on academics over athletics as a way to increase financial awards is a strategy that is endorsed by the president of the NCAA, Myles Brand. In a *New York Times* article titled "Expectations Lose to Reality of Sports Scholarships," he writes:

> *"The real opportunity is taking advantage of how eager institutions are to reward good students. In America's colleges, there is a system of discounting for academic achievement. Most people with good academic*

records aren't paying full sticker price. We don't want people to stop playing sports; it's good for them. But the best opportunity available is to try to improve one's academic qualifications."

Sometimes I get top high school or club players who think that their **athletic** talent alone will get them admitted. In fact, in a D-III environment, it's their **academic** talent alone that will. Sports are really no different than music or artistic talent. They are a plus, but won't carry the day by themselves.

Kathleen Connell, Head Coach, Women's Basketball, Pomona College

So now you see that money is indeed awarded for academic credentials.

To increase your chances of getting a merit financial award, find a school where the most recent incoming freshmen class had grades and test scores that are below your child's grades and test scores. ***This may be one of the only strategies for the kid who has less than stellar academic credentials to get a non-athletic scholarship.*** Targeting schools below your child's academic standing may also address any concerns you have that the academic load will be too demanding if your child also participates in the sports program. D-III schools offer merit scholarships on the basis of grades and test scores because they want to attract better students. Regardless of how good a student your child is, they are more likely to get a healthy merit scholarship at a school where they are at the top end of the academic spectrum.

THE INSIDE TRACK

Here's a little tip: one strategy for getting more money from a school that doesn't offer athletic scholarships is to look for a school whose academic standards are somewhat below your child's credentials.

Academics Pay Off—Big Time

Olivia was a soccer player with good academic credentials. She wanted to play for a college with strong academics and a national reputation, but her family had no way to pay for an expensive education. Since Ivy League schools offer no athletic scholarships and/or merit money, she focused her efforts on private liberal arts schools that offer merit scholarships. Most of the schools she looked at were highly competitive, with acceptance rates in the 20 to 50 percent range. Her safety school was a local college with good academics but with more of a regional reputation than a national one. The acceptance rate there was about 72 percent. Olivia was admitted to all but one of the schools she applied to, but the difference in financial aid packages was huge. The regional school offered her their highest merit scholarship—$15,000 per year. She was also eligible to apply for additional scholarship money based on her major. And her family was eligible for need-based financial aid. In the end, she was awarded $23,000 per year of the $33,000 cost of attending the school and she chose to go there. ■

Also, you are not limited to what the school is willing to give you—you can explore other outside sources. There are many scholarships available outside of the colleges that are offered by community groups, corporations, national organizations, and on and on. Check out websites like www.FastWeb.com and www.Petersons.com to get an idea of what's out there. Your child will have to fill out applications and write essays for most of them, but there's no harm in asking your kid to put a little effort into this as part of the bargain.

A Subtle Difference with Not-So-Subtle Implications

There is another difference between D-I and D-III scholarship money. Because D-I scholarships are athletic scholarships, the recipients **must be participating in athletics** to continue receiving their scholarships. It's the college student's version of the proverbial "golden handcuffs." If a kid is happy in the sports program, there's no problem. If not, s/he is stuck, and leaving the team means giving up the scholarship or transferring and sitting out for a year.

I know plenty of D-I coaches who are stuck with girls on the team who have lost their passion for the sport but are still playing because if they quit, they will lose their scholarship.

Amy Bryant, Head Coach, Women's Tennis, Emory University

If your child gets money from a D-III school, it will be need-based, merit-based, or community-service-based, and is not contingent on him or her continuing to participate in athletics. If a kid is unhappy in a D-III athletic program and decides to stop participating, it won't affect his or her scholarship status. Staying the course once s/he has made a commitment to the athletic program is important; however, it's nice to know there is no financial punishment if everything doesn't work out as planned.

What really makes Division III great is the kind of student-athletes that come in. The students are there because they want to be, not because they're afraid they'll lose their scholarship. Then, mix in the student-athletes that are earning difficult degrees at the same time, and it makes it a lot more impressive.

James Akita, Head Coach, Men's Track and Field and Cross Country, Elmhurst College

---

This is not to imply that a D-III merit scholarship is preferable to a D-I athletic scholarship. In all likelihood, the D-I athletic scholarship will be more money and probably come from a school with a more competitive sports program. If your child is offered a D-I athletic scholarship to a school at the top of the list, consider yourselves among the lucky ones. But if the offer of an athletic scholarship results in your child attending a school that you have reservations about, there may be trouble down the road.

So What Does It All Mean?

Don't close off any of your options until you know what the schools can offer you. There are sources of money that can come into play besides traditional athletic scholarships. Initially, put your efforts into picking the schools that are the best fit. If it's the perfect place for your child, give the school a chance to try to work something out. A full ride at a school where your child will be unhappy could end up being a very short ride.

Encourage your child to be as appealing as possible via grades, test scores, community service, and extracurricular activities. It will open up a broader range of athletic options, and may give him or her sources of funding as well. It will also narrow the competitive field. Keep in mind that colleges are looking for depth, not just breadth. Some kids have a laundry list of activities but offer little evidence that they put much effort into any of them. Colleges are looking for signs of leadership and commitment within the activities students have pursued, so if your list of extracurricular activities is a little sparse but you can show time, effort, and leadership, colleges will look positively on that. For most high school athletes, the demands of participating in high school sports reflect positively on their commitment and leadership during the college application process. If you're interested in a school that doesn't offer athletic scholarships, or at least doesn't offer one to your child, make sure you ask what other forms of financial aid are available through that school. The schools vary widely on what they can offer. Make no assumptions—always ask.

Finally, don't prioritize your list of schools based on money offered; instead, prioritize it by fit. If you have a few schools that feel right, chances are at least one of them will be able to put together a financial package that will work for you. Too many families approach this by deciding they will send their child to whatever school gives them the most money (regardless of fit). If you look for the money first, and then force the fit based on that, get ready to be dealing with a transfer a year later.

·KEEPING SCORE·

✔ Assess what kind of financial aid is available at the schools on your list by looking at their websites and using some of the college guidebooks that have this information available.

✔ Go through the list again and indicate how selective the schools are, noting that generally the more selective schools can be stingier with their financial aid.

✔ Try to determine how your child's grades and test scores stack up to the most recent incoming class at each school to get a sense of how likely your child will be to get a merit scholarship.

✔ Look at your kid's high school activities and make sure there is at least one thing that demonstrates commitment and leadership.

CHAPTER 9

TWO FINAL LITMUS TESTS FOR YOUR COLLEGE LIST

A t this point, you should have a pretty finely honed list of "best fit" colleges for your student-athlete. Hopefully, you have about five to ten on your list. There are two last criteria of fit you can apply to each school as a litmus test to make sure it belongs on the list:

1. Would your child be happy and fit in well at this school *even if they didn't play their sport?*

Bottom line, stuff happens. The school choice must be one your kid could live with even if s/he had a career-ending injury. You should encourage your child to think about whether or not a school that s/he would not be happy at without their sport should be on the consideration list at all. Injury aside, kids choose to leave sports for lots of reasons. They may not be happy with the program/coaching staff/other players/playing time or any other aspect of the athletic program, they may just outgrow their desire to play, or their academic commitments may become more pressing and more important over time. You can include a few schools that are not as appealing without their sport. It's easy to overlook shortcomings of the school when your kid is enamored with the sports program. Just make sure the list also includes several schools that your child could be happy at without their sport. If you've done a good job with the academic credentials section and the non-athletic college priorities section, you should have some.

Disappointed but Doing Fine

Missy is the daughter of a woman who works with my husband. She was an outside hitter all of the years she played club and high school volleyball. She chose her college based on the competitiveness of the volleyball program, but also on the academics and her positive feelings about the campus and students after a visit. She did not play much her freshman season, which was expected. She played more in her second season, but as a center, not an outside hitter. She knew there were stronger players ahead of her in her usual position, so that was okay. What made it all start to unravel was her coach who got in a player's face and used pressure to motivate. Even though Missy had observed her coach's style all of freshman year, it felt different when she was the recipient of it. She had always responded better to coaches who were encouraging, not intimidating. She stopped enjoying the game and quit the team at the end of her sophomore year. Missy chose to stay at the school because it was a good fit for her, even without volleyball. Losing her sport was unfortunate but not a deal breaker. ▪

2. Are You Comfortable with the Level at which Each Program Operates?

Let's assume your child has a list of five to ten schools. They may all be in one division or may be from multiple divisions. Generally, you know it's going to be tougher to be recruited for a D-I program than a D-III program, but how do you figure out just how good any individual program is within one division?

In D-I, certain conferences are considered stronger than others, and within any conference, you can check the standings of any of the individual teams. For example, in basketball and football, the general consensus is that the following conferences are the strongest: Atlantic Coast (ACC), Big Twelve, Big East, Big Ten, Pacific Ten (PAC10), and Southeastern (SEC). They are also familiar because they are reported on in the media extensively. But D-III is a little more complicated because there are one hundred more schools than in D-I, there is little familiarity because there is no media coverage, and the conference pecking order is not as established. How important is it to your kid that the team s/he ends up on...

- ✧ **Is strong within D-III (has a chance of playing in the post season)**
- ✧ **Has a winning record**
- ✧ **Is competitive within the conference they belong to**
- ✧ **Has strong fan support**

To help explore the "standings" of the programs you are interested in, following are a couple of things I found useful:

To learn if a school has a winning record

Go to the school's website and click on the athletic page for your sport. There will be a link for statistics and you will be able to find a couple of years of history, including the team's wins and losses. You may have to scroll around a little to find the data.

To get a general ideal of where a school ranks for a given sport

Go to www.Masseyratings.com. From the home page, you can select any sport, either gender, and any level (high school, college, or pro). Then navigate to any division/level and get ratings. The site also has an in-depth explanation of how the ratings are derived, if you're interested.

To learn if a school is strong within D-III

Go to www.NCAA.com. Click on "Select a Sport," and then click on whatever sport you're interested in. Click on "rankings." If D-III rankings don't pop up, pull down "Select a Poll," and click on whatever D-III polls are available. This will give you the most recent top contenders. For example, if you look at men's basketball, you can see the top twenty-five D-III schools according to D3hoops.com.

For basketball, baseball, football, and soccer, you can drill even deeper. For these sports, there are specific websites devoted to D-III play: D3hoops. com, D3football.com, D3baseball.com, and D3soccer.com. On each of these websites, there is a link to a list of the top-ranked schools from the previous season and, typically, you can look back at the last five years. This will give you a good idea of which D-III schools have been the most competitive over time.

To learn if a school is competitive within the conference it belongs to

Go to the athletic page for the schools you're interested in and find out what conference they compete in. Be careful, as occasionally different sports will compete in different conferences. Then go to the webpage for that conference and click the link for your sport. It will show you the past season's rankings and win/loss record for each team in the conference. For your convenience, all of the D-III conferences are listed in Appendix A of this book, with the links to their websites.

To learn if the school has good fan support

The information available will depend on the sport and if attendance is tracked. If it is, you can find attendance numbers for D-I schools at www. NCAA.org, which will give you a good idea of how many people come to each game. For D-III schools, go to the website of the school you're interested in, link to the sport, link to the most recent season statistics, and check the box scores for specific games. The attendance will be listed. Pick a game or two that you know are big rivalries for that school to get a sense of how high attendance can get. To provide an example of the order of magnitude of attendance for one sport, Appendix B lists average attendance for the one hundred D-I schools, thirty D-II schools, and thirty D-III schools that have the highest average basketball attendance.

You can also find out the size of the venues by looking at the facilities link on the school's athletic page, but that only tells you how many the venue *can* hold, not how many usually attend. Other alternatives to check out are some of the student-written guidebooks. They tend to focus on the more well-known schools, so if you're looking at a tiny, unknown D-III school in a rural location, you probably won't find it in these books. *Students' Guide to Colleges: The Definitive Guide to America's Top 100 Schools Written by the Real Experts—The Students Who Attend Them* (phew!) has several student reviews of each college. In the "activities" section of these reviews, they will often comment about the role that sports plays at the college and the kind of fan support/attendance that sports gets. *The Insider's Guide to the Colleges* also has reviews, which sometimes include anecdotal information about sports and fan support. Even if this kind of information isn't available for the particular schools your child is interested in, these guides are easy and an engaging read for high school kids, and they will probably learn a lot of other things about the target schools.

One of the schools consistently contacting my son dropped off our list when we looked at its history and found that the team typically lost more than half of their games every season. Despite a promising new coach, my son wasn't interested. Some kids are fine with being on a team that has been struggling so they can help rebuild and improve the program; mine isn't one of them. The two litmus tests discussed in this chapter should help you refine your list a little bit more.

·KEEPING SCORE·

✔ **Present your child with a hypothetical example about a career-ending injury and see if that changes how they prioritize which schools they're interested in.**

✔ **Decide the importance of each of the listed criteria for the level a program operates at.**

✔ **For any that are high priority, follow the research steps to determine how each of the schools on your list measures up.**

✔ **Narrow your list accordingly and aim for a list of five to ten schools.**

10

STARTING THE RECRUITING PROCESS

I t helps to think of the process as having two distinct parts that can be addressed separately. The first part is the research on the colleges and sports programs that will result in your final list of schools to target. The second part is initiating communication with the coaches of the programs you're considering, and all the activities that will happen subsequent to that. You can start the initial research at any time—the sooner the better. And don't assume you can knock this out in a weekend. In an ideal world, this part of the process should actually start *freshman year* for a few reasons.

◆ As you've already read, any athlete who plays at the Division I or Division II level for an NCAA-sanctioned school must register with the NCAA Clearinghouse and submit grades and standardized test scores that meet their hurdles. While the process of registering doesn't have to happen until later in high school, your child must be aware of the course requirements they will need to qualify, and the best way to do this is to loosely chart their four-year course selection at the beginning of high school. For Division III players, it's not necessary to meet NCAA standards—just the school's standards, but at this point in the game, most kids don't know where they will end up playing.

◆ Don't wait until junior year to try to convince your child that good grades will broaden their college options, as it may be too late. If their freshman year grades are lacking, they will have a tough time bringing up their GPA.

◆ You will want to talk to as many people as possible about schools to consider. Coaches, counselors, teachers, and parents who have been through it before will all have interesting perspectives and stories to share. You can also take the opportunity to do campus visits if a college is conveniently located to your home or a relative or is near the location of a family vacation. And don't underestimate how much information you can find about the schools and sports programs on the Internet. These three activities can keep you occupied for years, not just weeks, so starting early makes sense.

THE INSIDE TRACK

Because most high school kids start their college search during junior year, student-athletes tend to do the same. Start earlier. You and your child have more work to do.

Also, throughout the high school years and during the summers, your child will probably be playing on off-season teams such as club and AAU leagues (more about that later), building a reputation, and getting exposure. If those competitions take them beyond your local area, that provides another opportunity to visit college campuses. Most kids can't wrap their minds around getting serious about colleges until junior year, but the groundwork should already be laid by then—junior year is the time to actually start executing. If your child is an elite athlete, coaches and recruiters will start the process by contacting

him or her, or their coaches, before junior year, but for most, two things will happen junior year that will kick your kid into gear:

> The high school s/he attends will probably start pushing to start the college search process, and as with most things teenage, the herd mentality will take over. When their friends jump in, they will too.

> This may be the first year s/he gets any meaningful playing time at the varsity level in his or her sport, so s/he will finally have stats and video to present to a college coach. Many kids will not have enough to show prior to junior year.

Oftentimes, athletes start their college search process during junior year, but researching schools that fit should be coming *to its conclusion* early in junior year. Your child should start taking whatever standardized tests s/he will need (ACT or SAT) during junior year, and if s/he plans to take any study/preparation courses in advance of the test, that needs to happen fall or winter of junior year.

Establishing contact with potential schools can happen as early as a student-athlete's freshman year through letters or e-mail. I would suggest for most D-III schools, toward the spring of their junior year, they should have been in contact with almost all the potential college coaches that they are interested in.

Bobby Van Allen, Head Coach, Men's and Women's Cross Country and
    Track and Field, Johns Hopkins University

The second part of the process is letting the coaches at the schools your kid is targeting know about your child. If s/he is not an elite prospect, early in junior year is probably good timing for this. If you're seeking information or looking to get some questions answered, any time is acceptable. Since s/he should now know the schools s/he is interested in, have your child send an initial letter of introduction to the coach with a promise to send stats when the season is over.

What if it's already senior year and you haven't gotten started? Are you too late?

It's never too late. Remember the story about Sarah at the beginning of the book? She started over at the beginning of senior year and was happy where she ended up. Many D-III kids don't get found until senior year. Sometimes the kid who was mediocre and not noticed as a junior has developed nicely as a senior and suddenly shows up on radar screens. Conversely, there may be someone a school was interested in six months ago who no longer looks as appealing to them, so a spot that they thought was filled may open up. Also, college teams may now be learning about a kid who plans to transfer, which opens up a spot. Be aggressive about contacting schools you're interested in and asking if they still have spots they need to fill. Even if they don't, they may be able to tell you who is still actively looking. Finally, while every school doesn't do this, some will bend the rules to allow late applications, if they're interested. Regardless of when you get started, just start the ball rolling. Part Three of this book will tell you what to do.

These two pages give you a timeline and an idea of when each of these activities should take place.

Freshman Year

✧ Plan out high school curriculum meeting NCAA Clearinghouse standards.

✧ Explore and join club/AAU teams; participate in showcase events.

✧ Start researching colleges and athletic programs online.

Sophomore Year

✧ Continue with club/AAU exposure events.

✧ Continue researching colleges and athletic programs.

✧ Talk to coaches, counselors, teachers, and parents to get advice and suggestions.

✧ Visit colleges if the opportunity presents itself.

Junior Year: First Half

✧ Generate your list of potential schools.

✧ Initiate contact with the coaches at those schools—let them know you're there.

✧ Take any study prep courses for the ACT or SAT.

✧ Take the ACT or SAT for the first time.

✧ Use vacation days to visit colleges to get a feel for different campuses.

Junior Year: Second Half

✧ Finish generating and narrowing your list of potential schools.

✧ Put together your mailing (Part Three, Chapter 12) and send it out.

✧ Retake the ACT or SAT.

✧ Use spring break for college visits.

✧ Register with the NCAA Clearinghouse.

✧ Ask your high school coach to write letters of recommendation to favorite schools.

Summer between junior and senior years

✧ Make more college visits to schools you're interested in.

✧ Continue with club/AAU exposure events.

✧ Attend a prospect camp at a school you're interested in.

✧ Attend showcases if your sport sponsors them.

Senior Year: Fall

✧ Get all of your applications out.

✧ Visit any other schools you're interested in and haven't been to.

✧ Go on official visits, if invited.

✧ Consider a second visit to any schools you're serious about.

✧ If nothing has materialized, re-contact schools you're interested in and/or contact some new ones.

✧ Continue attending showcases.

Senior Year: Winter

✧ Get the Free Application for Federal Student Aid (FAFSA) form filled out for financial aid. Filling out this application helps schools determine how much your family can reasonably contribute to your education and how much financial aid you will need.

✧ Apply for merit scholarships at the schools you're interested in.

To recap: Try not to wait until senior year. Fall of senior year is the time to be **_bringing closure_** by filling out the applications in the fall. Prior to that, you will have to go through the process of figuring out which schools make sense, marketing your child to them, and possibly getting exposure to colleges that are not familiar with your kid. Working backwards, there are good exposure opportunities the summer between junior and senior years, so all of the upfront research needs to happen before then. That doesn't mean it's impossible to make something happen after fall of senior year, but there will be fewer options as many kids have already made their decisions known. You will have to work with the coach to figure out how to get through the application process if you've missed the deadlines.

· KEEPING SCORE ·

✔ Start your research now; it's never too early.

✔ Go through the listed timeline and make sure you're on track with the activities that should already have happened.

✔ Look forward on the timeline to get a feel for what's coming ahead and start preliminary planning with your kid.

What's Next

So now you're ready to go to the next step. You have a great list of potential schools put together, and the next step is to *make sure that someone at those schools knows about your kid*. Time for marketing.

PART THREE

Getting Coaches Interested

CHAPTER 11

WHO DOES WHAT?

Before we talk about *how* to get your child noticed, let's talk about exactly *whose job it is* to make it happen. If you learn nothing else from this book, please take away this one truth: *you (and your child) are the ones who are responsible for this*. You can ask others for help and you may even find yourself paying others to help, but no one else will have the investment in your child's well-being that you will.

> ✧ **Too many parents wait for high school coaches or club/AAU coaches to take the lead.**
>
> ✧ **Too many parents wait for college coaches to find their kid.**
>
> ✧ **Too many parents wait too long because they just don't know what to do.**

When I interviewed the parents of the student-athletes whose stories are in this book, the majority of them commented that one of the biggest mistakes they made was assuming that high school coaches would take care of recruiting or that college coaches would find their kids. You need to keep the monkey on your back. Accept that you are the ones responsible for your child's recruiting. You may get help from coaches, counselors, and recruiting services, but no one can look after your child's best interests like you and your child. Don't wait for others to lead the effort, and whatever you do, don't sit around waiting to be found by college coaches.

Let's talk about high school coaches. There are all kinds:

⋄ Some will want to help and some won't be interested.

⋄ Some will have the time that's needed to help, some won't.

⋄ Some will have the knowledge about what to do, while others will be on shakier ground here.

⋄ Some will have the contacts that will help make it happen, some won't.

⋄ And some will think highly of your kid's talent, but not all will.

It's unrealistic to expect your child's high school coach to have the desire, time, knowledge, contacts, and warm fuzzies necessary to get your child recruited. Coaching a team, working, and spending time with their family probably take up the majority of a coach's time. You can and should get some help from your high school coach, but be realistic about what you can expect, and be grateful and gracious for anything the coach does for you. You may also find that if your child's head coach doesn't have the time to work with you, there may be an assistant coach in the high school program that has more time and is eager to get the experience of dealing with college coaches.

When kids take the initiative to make the contact, that tells the college coach that they're serious about their program, or at least have done enough investigating to be considering it. Coaches at your top choice schools should be told that their school and sports program is one of your child's top choices because coaches know that the likelihood of attending is much higher if they're a first or second choice, and they may go to bat for your child if their admissions department is amenable. Finally, since D-III coaches don't have the budget to be everywhere recruiting, they might not find out about your kid if you don't initiate the contact.

THE
INSIDE
TRACK

No one is obligated to help you, and worse, there is no guarantee that those who do offer assistance know what they're doing.

Seventy-five percent of student-athletes contacted us first. It's not because we don't go looking, but it's much more trouble to see potential recruits at a tournament, track down who they are, and find their coach, only to find out they're not interested.

Suzette Soboti, Head Coach, Women's Soccer and Lacrosse,
    University of Redlands

Unless you have college coaches watching you play when you are in ninth or tenth grade, you will most likely have to contact colleges yourself. There are a lot more unsigned seniors every year in January than there are early commitments in the fall.

Peter Cosmiano, Head Coach, Volleyball, Mississippi College

College Recruiting Has Changed

There is another reason why your child's high school coach may not be the person to rely on to get your child recruited. College sports recruiting *is a different animal than it was just a short time ago,* so even a high school coach who played the sport in college and is only ten years older than your child probably had much different recruiting experiences than your child will, making it tougher to guide you and your child through the process. Here are some of the differences:

The absolutely explosive presence of off-season (non-high-school) competition in many sports. AAU and club sports have changed recruiting in several ways:

◆ They provide unique exposure opportunities to be seen by many more college coaches. Since competition takes place off-season, college coaches have more time and freedom to attend these events for scouting purposes—time they typically don't have when their own teams (and high school teams) are competing. During high school competition, it's a big deal when there's a college coach in the house. During AAU and club competition, it's not unusual to have dozens of college coaches in attendance. This can work for you or against you. A great one-time showing can get a kid an offer that would never have materialized otherwise, but a poor showing at the one game or match the college coach attends probably negates all the influence of a high school coach who knows your child normally plays better and tries to make the case for you. Here's a case in point:

Overcoming a Bad Season

Our friend Nate is a basketball player who played AAU for several years. During the all-important season between his junior and senior years, he didn't play up to his usual. He was pretty bummed when he received no offers that fall. But Nate's senior high school basketball season was another story. He played his heart out. He was the leading scorer on his team, outscoring two players over seven feet tall who both had D-I offers coming from everywhere. Even with the help of his high school coach, it was tough for Nate to get any serious attention because the coaches who had seen him play AAU that summer were hesitant to reconsider. He was finally offered a D-II scholarship by a school whose coach saw him play for the first time at a showcase in March of senior year. Never underestimate the impact of off-season competition. ■

◆ If you're not participating in off-season competition, you may be at a disadvantage because spots will go to those the coaches are familiar with, even if they're not necessarily the best candidates.

◆ Off-season competition gives you a better perspective on just where your kid fits because now you can see them playing at what is usually a more competitive level, so you can get an idea of just how good they really are.

◆ In addition to the high school coach, club sports give college coaches an alternate source for recommendations. Some will rely heavily on high school coaches, but others will shift their "recruiting ear" to club and AAU coaches.

Coaches having personal access to kids via their cell phones and e-mail

A coach who is interested in a prospect will still want to develop a relationship with the parents as well, but before cell phones and e-mail, a coach was forced to communicate with the family via phone or letters, and parents could gate-keep the process more than they can today. Now a coach can communicate with your kid without your knowledge, and coaches are quite skilled at being persuasive with impressionable seventeen- and eighteen-year-olds. You lose some of your ability to safeguard and protect your child's interests.

Kids are getting scholarship offers in middle school

Coaches are targeting younger and younger kids. The oral commitments they get from thirteen-year-olds may or may not stick five years later, but they're recruiting blue chippers younger and younger. The point is that they find the strongest candidates and potentially more of their scholarship spots will be filled earlier and earlier. If your child hasn't been noticed by the time s/he is a junior, s/he can probably still play, but you may want to re-assess where you think s/he will fit and how to target those schools.

Personal camcorders put the potential to shoot game tape into the hands of everyone

There is no excuse for not having video footage to send out to interested coaches if your child participates in a sport where that's expected. You can shoot it yourself (or hire someone else to shoot it), and your own footage will clearly focus on your child. Even if you don't have a video camera, check with your school to see if they videotape athletic events. While the focus won't be just on your child, they will still probably let you make a copy. Video is a commodity these days, and without it, you are at a disadvantage.

The Internet makes it much easier for both sides to learn about the other

You and your child can research specific schools, their sports programs, the coaches, the roster, and what other students have to say about campus life there. Conversely, kids are cavalier about what they post about themselves on social networking sites, and coaches can learn a lot about the character of your kid from what is posted on these sites. When you're serious about sending information to coaches, have your kid check their Facebook and MySpace pages and clean them up. Offer your help with this; you may be a better judge of what could seem inappropriate to a coach.

• KEEPING SCORE •

✔ Recognize that it's time to roll your sleeves up and get it done.

✔ Encourage your kids to get anything questionable about them off of the social networking sites.

✔ Have a conversation about the calls, e-mails, and texts your child is getting from coaches. Make sure your child knows that you're available to them to discuss anything that seems inappropriate or makes them uncomfortable.

CHAPTER 12

MARKETING YOUR CHILD

H ere's the rub—you now have a big job to do that will also slow down the college application process for your kid. If you have determined that your child's happiness in college will be contingent on his or her ability to compete in their sport at the varsity level, and the recruiters aren't beating a path to your door, *you will have to create demand by marketing your child to the coaches at the schools on the list you have just created.* The schools that are responsive to your efforts and show some interest in your child are the ones that you need to explore further. There are several ways to get exposure for your child, and all will take time and/or money on your part.

Many people approach this process too passively. As some of the stories shared previously in this book have illustrated, athletes often wait to be found. Even if that ends up to be a successful strategy for some people, it creates an overwhelming sense of powerlessness, so just start doing something. Don't wait for the knight on the white horse to show up; get on the horse yourself.

The first marketing consideration is the type of sport your child participates in because different sports have unique marketing challenges. At the risk of oversimplification, I have broken down the types of sports into three broad categories.

Category 1: **_Team Sports_** such as basketball, baseball, field hockey, football, ice hockey, lacrosse, soccer, softball, volleyball, and water polo. This category includes the revenue-generating sports of basketball and football, and those sports, in particular, get lots of attention. (There are also isolated cases where another sport, such as ice hockey, is a revenue draw for a school.) Marketing your child in these sports is probably the most difficult because even though there are individual stats, each player's performance is dependent on the performance of the rest of the team. Other dynamics also come into play, such as leadership, selfishness vs. selflessness, chemistry with other players, flexibility with positions, communication with the coaches, and quality of the competition, etc. It becomes difficult for a coach to compare two players' stats from different teams because the dynamics of each team will have such a great influence on those stats. In these cases, videotape is important, and if someone from the coaching staff can observe in person, they learn that much more about all the intangibles. Give them this opportunity by sending schedules of where and when your child is competing.

Category 2: **_Subjective, Mostly Individual Sports_** such as badminton, fencing, gymnastics, tennis, diving, and wrestling. These are sports where players are competing as part of a team, but their actual performance is individual and therefore not as influenced by team dynamics. In these sports, the athletes sometimes have individual state or national rankings and they may have head-to-head competitions. While there is ample opportunity to compare them directly to others, the rankings or success rate generally still depend on the strength of the competition. It would be important here to market yourself based on how you compare to others head-to-head as opposed to your team's performance against other local teams. Finally, since these are typically not the revenue-generating sports, these coaches may not have recruiting budgets that allow extensive travel so it becomes imperative for you to get your information into their hands.

Category 3: **_Objective Individual Sports_** such as bowling, cross-country, golf, swimming, and track and field. These are considered objective because performance is measured similarly no matter who you are playing against or where you are playing, and it is not subject to judgment. Athletes involved in these sports are probably the easiest to market because the time or the score can be compared across players from all over the country. However, these are also not revenue-generating sports so you must gct this information into the hands of the decision makers.

These descriptions of different categories of sports should give you a starting point for thinking about what needs to be communicated to a college coach. Marketing your student-athlete can be accomplished by systematically working through several steps, all of which can be done by you and your child.

Marketing Strategy 1:
Fill Out the Questionnaires on the Schools' Websites

This is an easy way to get started and something kids can do on their own. Here is what they should do: use the search engine of their choice to locate the athletics section of the schools on your list, and go directly to your sport. You will find a prospective athlete questionnaire that can be filled out and submitted online. The questionnaires are all relatively similar from school to school so once you have all the information pulled together (test scores, grades, stats), you can zip through a lot of them in a short amount of time. This should at least get you on some mailing lists and start the ball rolling. Because this is such an easy activity, you should start this very early in the process and don't be afraid to send out to a lot of schools. On the other hand, recognize that because it's so easy and can be done by anyone regardless of skill, a million other kids will also be filling these out. Don't have high expectations on getting recruited based on this one activity. It's a way to get your feet wet and to get past the inertia of not knowing how to start.

Marketing Strategy 2: Send Out a Mailing

You should now have a target list of 5-10 schools that was compiled by using the criteria from the first half of this book. Send a mailing to the head coach for your child's sport at each school.

How do you find contact info for the schools?

You can get this information on your own. It's easy to find, and here's how:

If you want an exhaustive listing in hard copy, go buy *Peterson's Sports Scholarships & College Athletic Programs.* It compiles five hundred pages of program listings in one place. But my personal recommendation is that you step into the twenty-first century and look for everything you need at the schools' websites. Go back to the same web page where you found the prospective students questionnaire and you will find names and contact information (e-mail and phone) for the entire coaching staff. You will also find a mailing address to send your information to.

There are a few reasons I recommend using the schools' websites. First, some kids take the initiative to research schools on their own and some don't. If yours is the kind that doesn't, asking them to go to a number of schools' athletic pages to find the contact info for coaches will probably result in them looking around to see what else is there. Once they're on the school's athletic page, they will get curious about the team, the coaches, their stats, their conference, and anything else that shows up. Each school's website feels a little different and communicates both specific information and some subtleties about that school's program. A little web surfing may result in your child thinking a little harder about which schools look interesting and which don't. At the very least, it will encourage your kid to take a little more ownership of the process.

And second, published directories of contact information are out-dated before they even get into your hands. When we were trying to figure out which schools to target, we put together a tentative list of twenty-five to thirty schools and ran them by our high school coach. He added a few. Then we put the mailing together. Right before we mailed them out, I did one last check to confirm names and contact information. About six weeks had elapsed between the time we put the initial list of contacts together and when we were actually ready to send out the mailing. In that time, there were three head coaching changes on my list of thirty.

Okay, back to your mailing. You should be able to put together a list of five to ten schools with head coach names and contact information. This mailing should go out some time during junior year at the latest. It should include at least some of the following items:

A cover letter

This should come from your child and should show some knowledge of the school, sports program, and coach. Notice that the example below includes the team name and the name of the school within the text. A form letter that looks like it was sent to multiple schools won't warm a coach's heart. You should also include something about your athletic accomplishments. In the example, this student-athlete talks about his team's participation in the state tournament, and his personal accomplishments in that tournament. Finally, make sure to acknowledge your interest in the school, not just the sports program. Here's an example letter from a fictitious basketball player:

John Smith • 312-123-4567 (home) • 312-234-5678 (cell) • Johns@yahoo.com

---

4/20/08

Coach Bob Jones
Andrews University
New York, NY 12345

Dear Coach Jones:

I am writing to express my interest in playing basketball for the Tigers. I am currently a junior at Madison High School in Chicago, Illinois. This past season as a varsity starter, I was front and center for the most successful basketball season in our school's 43-year history. Our 27 and 7 team finished fourth in the state tournament. I was honored as all conference and all area honorable mention, and I was both a top-ten scorer and rebounder in the state tournament.

I am interested in Andrews because it has both a commitment to a strong basketball program and the academic standards that I am looking for.

Attached is a resume that details my academic and athletic accomplishments. I am also including additional stats, newspaper articles, and game tape from my junior season.

I am always trying to improve my game and consider myself a fast learner. I know I would represent Andrews in the most positive way. I hope you will consider me as a future Tiger and will look forward to starting a dialogue with you about 2008/2009. Good luck next season.

Sincerely yours,
John Smith

Student resume

It should include a photo, contact information, school information, academic standing and honors, athletic honors and brief stats, coach contact, and any additional references. Here is an example:

John Smith
Power Forward
Class of '08

Insert a photograph of your child here—try to have them in uniform showing their #

Contact Info:
100 Brookfield Way
Chicago, IL 60612
312-123-4567 (home)
312-234-5678 (cell)
Johns@yahoo.com(John's e-mail)
Parents@yahoo.com(Parent's e-mail)

DOB: 3/12/90   Height: 6' 8"   Weight: 240 lbs.   Vertical: 31"

ACADEMIC

School: Madison High School • Chicago, Illinois • 312-825-1100

This four-time U.S Dept. of Education Blue Ribbon Award winner has 4472 students and has been ranked as a top 100 high school in America by *Newsweek* and *U.S. News and World Report*.

GPA: 4.1 weighted, 3.4 unweighted   **Class Rank:** 384/4472
ACT: 30   **Honors:** National Honor Society
SAT: (add this, if applicable)   **Counselor:** Mary Jones, ext. 284

HIGH SCHOOL BASKETBALL

Coach: Coach Tom Jeffries, ext. 229

Awards:
First Team All Conference in the Midstate Conference 2006/2007
All Area Honorable mention 2006/2007
Team record of 27-7
Team leader in rebounds
4th Place in Illinois State Tournament
Allstate Insurance *Player of the Game*
Midstate Conference *All Academic Team*
Cook County *Scholastic Achievement Award*
2006/07 stats: Summary of statistics attached

REFERENCES

AAU Coach: Bob Lincoln, Midstate Stars, 312-876-5432
Teacher: Jane Levitt, ext. 238
Parent Coach: Jay Reno, 312-595-8364

Game tape

There are debates about both the content and timing of what you should send. Most everything I read (and my own instincts) suggests that for team sports, game tape—that is, uninterrupted and large chunks of a game—are much more useful than highlight tape. Even a mediocre player can string together great moments. That doesn't tell a coach anything about a kid's typical game demeanor, leadership ability, endurance, awareness of surroundings, team member support, and attitude on the bench.

Be selective about the game or games you put on the tape. It takes a coach a millisecond to size up the competition on your tape. A great showing by your kid against a team that is really weak tells them very little. Look for a decent showing against decent competition.

You also have to decide when to send it, and there are differences of opinion on this as well. If you include it in your mailing, the coach will have everything they need to determine how interested they are in you. You will speed up the process and will only need to send out one mailing. You may also choose not to include game tape in this first mailing, but let coaches know that it's available if they're interested. This will encourage them to initiate contact with you if they see anything in your mailing that piques their interest. This will also save you the time and money of making a tape for every school you're sending out to. Imagine how many tapes a typical college coach receives and, realistically, how many they actually look at. They will only review your tape if they see something in the supporting materials you sent that makes you look appealing, and if that's the case, they will request a tape be sent anyway. If you decide not to send out a tape in the first mailing, just make sure you have enough information in your packet to generate interest in your child.

Getting the tape made is no day in the park. You may need to invest in some professional help. We made ours using the resident software on our Apple laptop but I would be lying if I said it was easy; it took a month of trips back and forth to the Apple store. Check to see if your high school athletic department videotapes games or matches. If not, you may have to do some taping yourself or hire someone else to do it. Make sure to include something at the beginning of the tape indicating who your child is, what their number is, and what color their uniform is. Uniforms will change colors depending on whether you are playing a home or away game, so be aware of which you're sending. Back on the topic of highlight tape, another reason not to send any unless requested is that if you think game tape is hard to edit, just try creating highlight tape. Unless you're willing to pay someone else who is experienced at it, let it go at game tape.

Find out from the coaches at the schools you're interested in what they'd like from you and get it to them ASAP. For example, I cannot give feedback to a field hockey player until I have seen her play or have a video, and other field hockey coaches and I like a certain type of video. It need not be complicated—just ask us!

Elizabeth Walkenbach, Director of College House Programs, Former Head Coach, Field Hockey, Franklin and Marshall College

---

Other things to add to your mailing:

⬦ **Junior year or club team stats if you have them. Your high school coach or club team coach will be able to provide these for you if you had any meaningful playing time.**

⬦ **Copies of relevant/positive newspaper articles that may have been written about your child.**

⬦ **Schedules of where your child will be playing for the next six months.**

Don't be surprised if the phone doesn't start ringing three days after you send all of this out. Give it a week or two, and then follow up with a quick e-mail or note. Our experience was that some of the schools ignored it, but several did send back initial letters with athletic questionnaires and a few called. Most of those who called had seen or heard something about our son, but the mailing seemed to connect the dots and trigger the communication.

Here are some other important reasons to get your child's information to a coach:

First, when you take the initiative, it tells a coach that you're interested and that counts for a lot. You may also have an interest in several other schools, but coaches can live with that. It's their job to assess if their program and school is a good fit for you and then try to convince you accordingly.

Second, if coaches have to find you, their job is much more time- and effort-intensive without even knowing whether you would have any interest in them. Here's an example: a coach attends a club volleyball or soccer tournament to observe a lot of kids at once. Every kid on each team comes from somewhere else. Now the coach has to figure out where the specific kids they're interested in come from and how to best contact them. It may be through the club team coach or it may be through the high school coach. Not all high school coaches are affiliated with the school where they coach (they may have a full-time job elsewhere) so they may be difficult to locate. And the coach has to do all of this without having any idea whether the kid has any interest in the school. Lots of effort—slim chance of payback. It's so much easier for a coach to start with a universe of kids who have already expressed interest in the school and the sports program.

Third, many schools don't have the recruiting budgets to travel outside of their region. The best programs don't have the need anyway, because they can find so many good players locally. This is even truer for sports that have traditionally been stronger in certain regions than others. If you play one of these sports, you will have to toot your horn loudly to be heard, and you should probably start earlier—freshman or sophomore year—so these coaches can follow your progress the same way they're following the progress of more local players.

Everyone wants to be wanted. Coaches are no exception.

Trumped by Local Players

Jamie and Bob both live in the Chicago suburbs. Jamie is a water polo player and Bob plays lacrosse. Their attempts to get the attention of college coaches taught this lesson: that you need to consider the regional nature of recruiting in your sport. Following are their stories.

Jamie was a three-sport athlete—football, swimming, and water polo. He would have pursued any one of these in college. His parents weren't that crazy about football, and even though he had good swimming times he had to admit that he enjoyed water polo the most. He had four Division I California schools high on his list, primarily for the programs they offered in his academic area of interest. He looked at water polo at these schools and discovered he was on a short list of non-local athletes contacting them. The coaches typically recruit local athletes whose careers they have been following for several years. Water polo programs are not as long-standing in the Midwest as they are on West Coast. Despite Jamie's talent, the coaches didn't know enough about him or the programs he had played in to be comfortable recruiting him. If he is admitted to one of these schools, he can be a walk-on, but there are no guarantees and there is no scholarship offer.

Bob was the goalie on the varsity lacrosse team for four years and a team captain. The number of high schools in the Midwest that field a lacrosse team has grown dramatically over the last ten years, but the programs still have a long way to go to catch up with their counterparts on the East Coast. Bob wanted to play college lacrosse, but he knew that the competition would be intense, especially at the elite, small liberal arts schools where lacrosse is much more popular than football and coaches scout local talent for years, especially goalies. During one of Bob's many campus visits, he found a school where he knew he would be happy—whether or not he played lacrosse. He was accepted early-decision, and even though there are three recruited goalies on the roster, he will show up and try out with no expectations. ■

Fourth, and probably the single most important reason why you should actively get your information in front of a coach is this: *unless you are an elite athlete, you are part of a large group of interchangeable competition, and you need to find a way to stand out so that you won't be lost in the shuffle.* Let me try and illustrate what I mean. The following graph is the standard bell curve that you probably remember from school. The horizontal axis shows athletic ability and the vertical axis shows number of kids. The bell curve implies that most kids cluster at average ability, some are low ability, and some are high ability. The least amount of kids are at either end (very little ability, elite athlete). Detail A shows where most athletes and their parents see themselves relative to the kids they compete with in high school—at the top end of the curve.

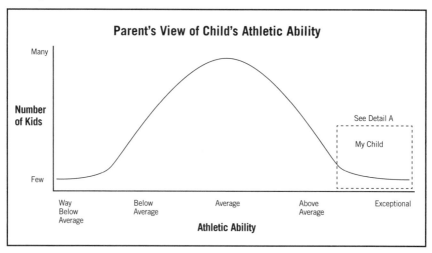

But college coaches don't concern themselves with the athletes on most of this curve—only the ones at the far right end. Their world is only what's in the box labeled Detail A, and it looks a little more like the next graph:

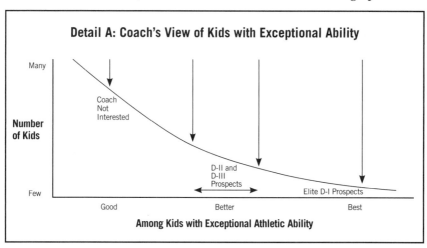

Coaches are only looking at kids at the very end of the bell curve. The further your child falls on the right toward elite, the less competition s/he will have. *But as you can see, as they move more toward the left, the number of kids they have to compete with for spots increases exponentially.* At least some of these kids will be a good fit and will have the academic credentials to get admitted to the schools that your child is interested in. Marketing your child and getting him or her in front of this coach may make all the difference.

Marketing Strategy 3: Ask People Who Matter to Make Calls

Put yourself in a coach's shoes. Who are they going to trust? Your mailing will have lots of relevant information but it's coming from a nonobjective source. If you have a small list of schools you're really interested in, ask people who know your child's skills, and more important, have credentials that would make them a credible source, to make some calls on your behalf. This can be your high school coach, club coach, a current athlete at the school, an alumnae who is well connected with the school…the list goes on. Often, one phone call from a highly credible source will get you much further than all the mailing and personal exposure.

When we put together our list, our first mailing went to the school that was clearly on the top. The response we got was a fairly typical letter with the student athletic questionnaire enclosed for us to send back. After we sent this back, we received information about its summer prospect camp, but not much else. Then we ran into a trainer who had worked with my son years before. He was doing some summer training with a few of the guys who were on this college team already, and he thought our son would be a good fit in this program. He called the coach that night, and the coach called my son the next day. Our efforts may have started the ball rolling, but it was really his phone call that sealed the deal.

Marketing Strategy 4:
Have Coaches See Your Child Up Close and Personal

Have your child take advantage of some of the following ways to get exposure:

Off-season club or AAU teams

These are for kids who are serious about getting to the next level. They can hone their craft as they continue playing year round. These teams participate in high-profile tournaments that are frequented by college coaches. They may be coming to watch a particular athlete, but if they see your child at the right moment, that's all that matters.

Showcase events

These are usually one- or two-day events that can be entered as a solo (as opposed to with a whole team) and they are specifically for the purpose of getting exposure to coaches. The folks running it will probably take some measurements, lead them in drills, and have scrimmages. Your kid's "stats" from this event will be given to coaches who attend and some who couldn't but still want the information. There's a lot of showcase events—research them to determine which showcases will be attended by the kinds of schools you're interested in targeting. Whoever is sponsoring the showcase will be happy to give you the list of potential attendees. This may change twenty times before the event. Ask for the list of last year's attendees. That will be the best predictor of the kind of schools that will show up. There are showcases for specific positions, for strong academic candidates, and for unsigned seniors.

Prospect camps

These are camps that are offered on college campuses during the summer. They are a win/win. The school makes a little money (yes, you'll pay to attend) and the coach gets to see kids who are interested in playing at the next level and interested in their school in particular. Your kid gets to showcase his or her talents to schools that you're interested in. Kids who participate also get to see and feel what the campus and athletic facilities are like, and they work with the coaches, and possibly, some of the players. Much better than a blind date, both parties get some decent data points about each other with which to make some decisions. If a school has heard about your child and has some interest, they may send information about their camp and encourage your child to come, but anyone can go to these camps, so find out if the schools you're interested in run one. If they do, it's a no-brainer to attend. The timing of when to attend one of these camps is going to be dependent on what sport your child is in and when their season is. Talk to coaches about the best time to attend.

Not all schools run these camps, but when my son attended one at an Ivy League school (Division I), there were several Division III assistant coaches from nearby colleges who were hired to help as coaches at the camp. It turned out to be one of the best kinds of exposure he could have gotten. Since it was a different region of the country from where we lived, he was not well-known to these coaches. A good performance at this camp opened up his recruiting with a whole new group of schools. He ended up going to a school that was not at this event, but his second choice was one of the schools that found him at this camp, and the ironic part is that he stumbled into that situation without realizing the benefits.

Here's some advice about the camps: When you figure out the few schools you're most interested in, find out if they run a summer prospect camp and plan on attending. Go to the school's website and find the page for the sport your child plays. There will usually be a link to their summer camps if they offer them. Many colleges offer camps for little kids so make sure you're looking at a college prospect camp. If the schools you're interested in don't run a camp, contact the head coach and ask if they send anyone from their coaching staff to any area summer camps to help coach. If they do, go there. Alternatively, you can contact the folks who run the camps you're interested in and ask them to give you a list of the schools who helped the prior year.

You may also want to consider having your child attend one of these camps the summer between his or her sophomore and junior years. The downside is that kids who are average or barely above average athletes will have a tough time standing out in a field of kids who are older, stronger, and more experienced at the sport. The impression they create at this point may follow them around with the coaches that see them. On the other hand, if your child is talented enough to play well against older kids, getting out there early increases their exposure and gives coaches time to get familiar with your kid's skills. A coach may start a dialogue early on and watch your child through his or her junior year.

These numerous ways to be seen outside of the high school team are intended to drive home the point that you shouldn't limit play to the high school team.

Look at it from a college coach's point of view: attending high school games and matches will force a college coach to observe lots of kids who don't have the skills to play the sport at the college level. Attending club, AAU, showcase events, and prospect camps allow coaches to observe a much larger number of college-ready players. If you were in their shoes, where would you spend your time?

THE INSIDE TRACK

College coaches are becoming more dependent on non-high-school venues for prospecting recruits, and less dependent on high school sports.

Alternatives to Doing It Yourself

What if you get to the end of this marketing section and decide that you don't have the time/motivation/interest/competence to do what you have to do to get your child recruited? Despite all the "don't haves," if one thing you *do have* is extra money to burn, you can always try an athletic recruiting service. I personally don't have experience with them so I don't know how helpful they would be to you. Their critics say that they routinely inflate the skill level of their clients so coaches don't always believe them, and that they don't always give student-athletes the kind of attention they are paying for, but I bet the better ones have long lists of student-athletes they have placed in college programs so they must be doing something right.

The general drill is that, for a fee, they will post information and stats about your child on a website, and the services escalate from there. They can produce and distribute resumes and videotapes of your child. This could be useful if you don't have the time, equipment, or experience to do this (particularly the video piece). They can cost anywhere from a few hundred to a few thousand, depending on the services you need.

If you choose to go this route, my best advice would be to ask for several references and check them carefully. Find out exactly what was promised, what was delivered, if they received the attention they expected, and if they would use this recruiter for their next child. Stay away from services that promote kids regardless of their ability. College coaches won't put any credibility into their recommendations. A better bet would be services that provide you with a template for your resume, have a contact list, and offer you advice about schools which may be a good fit for you. But then again, most of that is available between the covers of this book for much less. Let the buyer beware.

What Should I Expect from AAU and Club Teams?

For many sports, such as basketball, volleyball, baseball, soccer, and ice hockey, club and AAU participation has been migrating to mandatory as opposed to optional. Unless your child is a world-class athlete that will develop and get noticed without this exposure, participation is becoming the cost of entry for continuing in the sport. There are pluses and minuses about these programs. They will certainly compete at a more advanced level than what is available at their high school, and presumably, playing against better competition should help athletes improve. Here is a list of the things *I can guarantee* will happen if you and your child choose to participate:

- ◆ I guarantee you will spend a lot of money. There is the cost of participation, which includes uniform and equipment, practice time and rental of space, coaches, and training, and that is only the beginning. The travel costs can dwarf the participation costs, particularly if other family members accompany the athlete. As the athlete gets older and the stakes get higher, the travel gets more far-ranging, i.e., more expensive.

- ◆ As a close corollary to the above, I guarantee you will spend a lot of your weekends in hot, sweaty gyms; on cold, windy, and muddy fields; or at freezing ice rinks. Only once in a rare while will you be in a reasonably family-friendly location like Las Vegas or Orlando. Most of the time, you will be spending what should have been your vacation dollars on budget hotels in places like Ft. Wayne, Des Moines, and Poughkeepsie.

◆ I guarantee you will enjoy the company of at least a few of the parents of the other athletes on the team and they will become your new best friends because you will spend inordinate amounts of time together in less than favorable conditions. You will also encounter some parents who should be locked up, or at least muzzled. A club team is like any community—you will like some parents and you will not like others. If the balance shifts too much to the latter, gently nudge your kid to join another team—there are plenty out there and life is too short.

And here's the bad part:

◆ I guarantee you will start to think that the least your child should get out of this is a college scholarship because you and your family have sacrificed so much money and time for this involvement. Sadly, this falls on the list of things that may happen but aren't guaranteed to happen.

The list of things that *aren't guaranteed* also includes the following:

◆ Your child may improve in both skill and understanding of the sport, but then again, maybe not. It stands to reason that if kids invest a lot of time and effort into a sport, they should improve. But this doesn't take into account that every person eventually hits a point where their skills stop developing, or their body stops growing. When my son was in sixth grade and 5'4", he played ball with a kid who towered over everyone at 5'11". He could hit lay-ups and collect rebounds all day long, but as a graduating senior, he was still 5'11". His skill set never really developed, and he was done with high school ball after sophomore year. Club/AAU teams can provide your child with practice, exposure, and skill development, but they can't fool Mother Nature.

◆ Kids can burn out and lose their passion for the sport. If this level of intensity starts at ten years old, they may grow to hate it by seventeen, and they may resent a parent's insistence that they stick with it.

◆ Your child may have trouble reconciling the club team role with the high school team role, and as a result, the high school experience may be less satisfying. High school programs may require more discipline, structure, and practice than club teams, and because there is no money involved in most high school sports, high school coaches don't have to deal with the demands and expectations of paying parents in the same way that club coaches do. I recently read an article with a great insight from a high school coach who said; *"Kids see how fun AAU is. They travel all over the country. They play a lot of games and probably don't have to prac-tice much. The AAU teams are feeding these kids candy and we're the ones yelling at them to eat their vegetables."* A comment a mother can really identify with.

♦ And as mentioned above, your kid may get a scholarship at the end of it all, but there are no guarantees. Sadly, many parents assume that a scholarship is the unwritten promise of club/AAU participation. Your investment in club/AAU sports does not come with payback in the form of a scholarship. There aren't enough to go around. It's fine to go into this hoping for a scholarship, but make no mistake, it's not an entitlement, and if your child doesn't get one, the club/AAU program is probably not 100 percent to blame.

THE INSIDE TRACK

Club and AAU teams can only put kids into a position to get the needed exposure—the athletes have to do the rest by having, and showcasing, the set of characteristics someone is looking for.

Having said all this, if you can afford these pro-grams, and if you can think about them as a way to invest in your child's well-being, there is a lot to gain—just not necessarily a scholarship. A father who was being interviewed in Bill Pennington's *New York Times* article about the amount of money he had invested over the years in club soccer for his two college-age sons commented on the perils of looking at the money spent as a financial trans-action with a payback at the other end:

"You are misguided if you do it for that reason. You cannot recoup what you put in if you think of it that way. It was their passion and we wanted to indulge that."

·KEEPING SCORE·

✔ Have your child fill out the athletic questionnaires on the websites of the schools on their list.

✔ Get up-to-date contact information from school websites.

✔ Before you do your mailing, get feedback from knowledgeable sources (coaches, trainers, counselors) about your list to make sure you aren't missing any obvious schools.

✔ Create a cover letter and resume for your mailing.

✔ Create a DVD of your child's performance. You may want to ask your top choice schools what they specifically want to see.

✔ Add statistics and newspaper articles about your child to the mailing.

✔ Add a schedule of where your child will be playing for the next six months.

✔ Mail it all out!

✔ Ask relevant people to make phone calls.

✔ Research the options for camps, showcase events, club/AAU teams and decide what you can afford.

✔ Have a conversation with your kid about realistic expectations for club/AAU participation.

PART FOUR

Getting Recruited

13

THE DANCE BEGINS

This chapter is written directly to kids because they will be participating in everything that happens from here on and need to know what to expect and how to handle it. For most of you, this will be your first experience with the recruiting process and you will feel out of your comfort zone. You're not sure what you're supposed to do, whether you should initiate or hang back, how to interpret the actions of those around you, when you're being dealt with honestly vs. when you're being lied to or strung along, and what to do when you're left high and dry. In other words, you don't know the rules of this particular game. If it sounds vaguely familiar, it's a road we've all been down before in a different context. ***Think of recruiting as comparable to courtship. Apply the rules of dating, and it will seem more logical and familiar.*** Bear with the continual analogy because it provides a frame of reference for understanding the basics of recruiting: there are two sides involved, both have agendas that are not necessarily clear to the other, and the relationship only works when the needs of each party can be met by what the other has to offer. Let's take a closer look at the steps involved.

The First Letters (Let's-Go-for-Coffee Date)

Regardless of which party initiates the relationship, the first communication from the sports program will probably be in the form of a letter to your child. It will outline a few choice words about their program and why your child should be interested. It will probably have a student-athlete questionnaire enclosed with an invitation to return this questionnaire. Your child may even receive this from a program s/he has already sent a completed questionnaire to. This is because someone other than the coaches manage the mailing list that these form letters go out to, even though coaches may have already received and read your questionnaire (classic example of the left hand not knowing what the right hand is doing).

THE INSIDE TRACK

Those initial letters will make your kid feel handpicked and special. S/he is not alone. Thousands of other kids will be enjoying the same letter.

This is like an initial blind date where you meet for coffee. The school got your child's name as someone who might have something to offer but they know very little and are just putting out an initial feeler. In fact, yours may just be a name they found on a list somewhere—this isn't even necessarily coming from a personal recommendation. Recently, I heard a presentation from an athletic director at a small (thirteen hundred undergraduates) Midwestern Division III college. When asked about these "letters," she said their first round of prospecting letters goes out to about two thousand high school seniors. This is across all the sports they sponsor, but you get the point.

These letters do not indicate serious interest or that they even know anything more about your kid than any other student-athlete on that list. They mean one thing only: ***We need to start creating our recruiting list for next year, so we're inviting you to let us know if you have any interest in being considered.*** If you want to stay on their list, send back the questionnaire. If it's not a school your child would ever consider, don't send it back. Some of them will take you off the list right away while others will keep wasting postage.

Early on, my son got a letter from one school that had a comical and unlikely error in the street name of our address. Over time, we noticed that he continued to get letters from that school as well as a few other schools that all had the same error. It was obvious that they had gotten his name off of some list that had screwed up the address. We realized that they knew nothing about him.

Initial letters may also come to your child's high school coach. You can take these a little more seriously. They would have to have seen or read about your child but not known how to contact him or her personally. While these initial letters do not indicate any serious interest, there are two other things to look for. Other than your name at the top, when you read the letter, you can usually tell if it's a standard form letter that could have gone out to anyone, or if there is something more personalized. If they mention having seen your kid play at a specific tournament or a high school game, or if the envelope has a typewritten or handwritten address, you can figure it's more serious than if it's clearly a one-size-fits-all form letter with a computer generated mailing label on the envelope. Also, this correspondence is another useful way of gauging exactly where your child may fit. What kinds of schools are they coming from? Are they coming from one division more than another? Do they tend to be only local/regional schools or has your child's name gotten out more broadly? Just make sure to remember that these letters are only their way of saying "hello."

Many recruits/parents do not realize that college coaches are recruiting sizable numbers of athletes. Parents don't realize that a form letter/e-mail does not make you a 'top recruit.' There are numerous letters/e-mails being sent.

Gerri Seidl, Head Coach, Women's Basketball, Carnegie Mellon University

---

One misunderstanding is that because a student receives general information from a college coach, the student-athlete assumes they are being recruited as a priority athlete.

Penny Siqueiros, Head Coach, Softball, Emory University

More Letters (Great! We Made It Past the First Date)

Let's assume you are interested enough in this school to send back the questionnaire. If it's a school you're really interested in, you should also send back some of the materials talked about before—give them as much about your child as possible so they can make an informed decision about continuing. Don't underestimate the value of letting a school know you're interested. Remember—in the dating game, everyone wants to be liked even if they don't end up with you. Your response lets them know the blind date was fine and now they have to decide if they really want to go out with you.

Maybe you'll begin a few weeks or months of casual dating. No strings or commitments yet—you are both getting to know each other a little better. This may go on for a while. There will be more letters back and forth and they may give you more specific information about them and ask for more about you. Some schools will start sending you motivational mailings about the successes their program has had. The communication venue may change—they may start e-mailing, text messaging, or even calling to check in on your child. This is an exciting time, especially if this is going on with several schools. Here are a couple of things to keep in mind:

Just like this stage in a real courtship, so far neither party is committed to the other. ***This means that as you're having these kinds of relationship-building activities with several schools, all of the schools that are talking to you are talking to many other people as well.*** You have no idea how many, but you should assume that they still have a lot of narrowing down to do.

Several of these schools will be new to you. You have the Internet at your disposal, so learn everything you can about the school and what they have to offer academically and athletically. Some of the things you can learn about the athletic program are obvious from looking at the team's roster.

> You will be able to tell if that school draws from an international, national, or local/regional base for their team roster. Division I schools usually draw from at least a national base. Some Division III schools also draw from a national base, but others draw from a local base.

> Are there players on the team who are transfers from junior colleges or are transferring in from other programs? Or are all the incoming players newbie freshmen like you? Does it make a difference to you?

> If you participate in a sport where physical size characteristics are important, such as basketball, football, and volleyball, are the height and weight characteristics of the players on the team similar enough to yours so that you could be reasonably competitive on this roster?

> Are the players evenly distributed across freshman/sophomore/junior/senior years, or are they more heavily weighted toward one end or the other? Again, does it make a difference?

> Is there a junior varsity team? (You will find this at some Division III schools.) Would you be okay playing JV for a year or would that be a deal-breaker?

Your child's high school probably has a college center or college counselors that can also help you research specific schools. You may be surprised to find that a program you never even heard of is a perfect fit.

It's always tough to cut short new relationships, but at the same time, if it doesn't feel right, it probably isn't. Cut your (and their) losses and don't string them along. After kids get over the initial ego boost of being sought after, having to figure out what to say to coaches they're not interested in will get old. And think of it from the coach's standpoint: if you take yourself out of the running, you're one less person a coach has to follow up with and try to figure out. Coaches are used to being broken up with early and often at this stage.

What should you say to those you're not interested in?

There's no point in being nasty or standoffish. Just like in any industry, these folks talk and compare notes, so offending one coach may get you on the "avoid" list of many others. If you're really not interested in a particular school, simply tell the coach that there are several schools you're talking to now that seem to be a good fit and you would like to pursue them first. Then, if it doesn't pan out, you would like to be able to re-contact them. No hurt feelings. This is similar to the "let's be friends" break-up. You both know you probably won't be friends in the long run, but it's a comfortable parting line for all involved.

Please be honest with me. I am the professional and the adult in this relationship. You may be contacting eight to twenty schools. I am contacting three hundred or more kids. I want to be the best recruiter I can be and develop a relationship as best as I can. Tell it to me straight when you're moving on. I can take it. If I can't, that's not your problem.

Elizabeth Walkenbach, Director of College House Programs, Former Head
Coach, Field Hockey, Franklin and Marshall College

Keep the coach updated on your level of interest. Regular updates go a long way. Likewise, if you are no longer interested, save everyone time and let the coach know.

Charles Griffiths, Head Coach, Swimming, Claremont-Mudd-Scripps Athletics

Setting limits

If your kid isn't getting much in the way of contacts, you will need to market them to different schools or recognize that maybe it's not meant to be. But what if the opposite is true? What if your mailbox is stuffed every day, your child's e-mail is full, and coaches are always text-messaging and/or calling your child? If they are the ones you're interested in, your kid probably loves it. But chances are there are several your child isn't interested in and is avoiding. It's tough for a kid to give the "let's be friends" speech to a coach. Help your child take control of the process instead of letting it control your kid. Set time limits for answering e-mails and talking to coaches, and set up a schedule for your child that includes homework time, workout or practice time, and whatever else needs attention. Advise your child to tell a coach that he can't talk because he's got to study to keep up the grades that all these fine institutions will require for admission. Crisis averted.

Watching You in Action (A Weekend Date)

Now they're interested enough to want to visit you for a more extended "look-see" at what you've got to offer. They've asked for your schedule and are coming to see you in a high school game, showcase event, off-season tournament, or whatever. They may also already have reviewed some video of you and liked what they saw enough that they want to see you in person.

This is like spending your first weekend together. They want enough exposure to you to know if there is any reason to continue this relationship.

Unlike dating, it's a little one-sided because they're doing all the learning about you and other than seeing who they are, you're not getting much of an education about them. Because of NCAA rules, they may be prohibited from talking to you at all when they come to see you. So many intangibles come into play when coaches can actually see you in action, so the in-person viewing is pretty important even if they've reviewed you on tape. You will have to wait for a campus visit to get the same "feel for them" in return.

The Campus Visit (Time to Meet the Parents)

Coaches don't exist in a vacuum. They come complete with assistants, players, facilities, training programs, campuses, and academic requirements. It's similar to the first time you realize your significant other comes with parents, siblings, friends, and a past life. For the relationship to continue, you have to decide how you feel about what baggage they come with—both good and bad. It's time for a campus visit. In Division I and Division II, recruited athletes are invited to come on an official campus visit paid for by the school. In Division III, recruited athletes make unofficial visits and pay their own costs. Some D-III schools will foot the bill but it's unlikely that they will

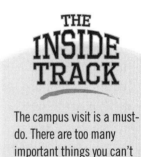

THE INSIDE TRACK

The campus visit is a must-do. There are too many important things you can't find out any other way.

advertise the fact, so it never hurts to ask. If you are the one initiating the visit and not the coach, you are probably not being recruited by this school.

Similar to the point in a relationship when you meet the parents, you are expanding your view of a relationship from what exists between you and your significant other to all of the things that will become part of your life together, for better or worse. Seemingly ideal relationships can be derailed at this stage. For example, religious, financial, or cultural differences may just seem insurmountable to the parties involved.

The campus visit presents an analogy in that not only do you have to like the coach and what you have come to learn about the sports program, you now get to decide how you feel about the campus, the other students, the academics, the location, the other team members, their style of play, the athletic facilities, and so on. If you find that there are parts of this picture you can't live with, you'll know this isn't the right fit for you.

One of the ways in which this process is different from the typical courtship process is that neither of you are monogamous at this point. You should be setting up campus visits at several colleges that look like they might be good fits for you. Be prepared to have an answer when the coaches ask you who else you're looking at—they all will. *At the same time, know that these coaches are probably looking at somewhere between four and six people for the one specific spot they're considering you for.* They have to. They don't know who is going to best fit with their program and school, they don't know if you have the credentials to get into the school, and, most of all, they don't know if you will choose their school or another one. At the end of this process, you will have a list of schools in some priority order in your mind from favorite to least favorite. Your agenda will be to get yourself onto the team of your first choice. The coaches all have a similar agenda. They have a list of individuals they're looking at for each position—called their depth chart—and it's also in order of favorite to least favorite.

The coach's 'recruiting game'—a school may be in contact with as many as 250-350 players per year, 40-50 seriously (handwritten notes and letters, the one call per week, etc.); 6-12 all-out; top 3-4 they will ask for early commitments.

Terry Liskevych, Head Coach, Women's Volleyball, Oregon State University

---

The early commitments referred to by Terry Liskevych is more typical of D-I scholarship offers, but some D-III coaches may encourage early decision applications in an attempt to accomplish the same objective of getting their next year's recruiting class in the books.

Here's the really hard part: *you don't know where you stand on their depth chart of favorite to least favorite.* Time to ask the really tough questions. Don't shy away from it—coaches need to be accountable to you so you can make an informed decision.

This point is like that stage of a relationship when you want to know where you stand. You're into it and you're not sure if you're dealing with your future spouse or a total commitment-phobe. You muster up the courage to ask something like: *Where is this going?* or *Do we have something here?* If you don't ask, you'll make assumptions that may make you feel good but are entirely unfounded. But if you do ask, you need to be ready to hear the answer and move on if that's where it leads you. Some coaches can answer honestly regardless of whether it's the answer you seek. Others can't and spin their answer for the comfort of everyone involved. Use your gut instincts to figure it out.

So back to the question about how many are on that depth chart and where you stand within that group. Just ask. Maybe you'll get an honest answer and maybe you won't. They will probably treat the fifth choice the same as the first choice so that won't help you figure it out. Since they don't know if their preferred choices are going to pick them or not, they have to protect themselves by treating everyone they're looking at as a kid that may end up there. If they told you that you were their fifth choice, you'd be high-tailing it to the interstate in a New-York minute. No one wants to be left at the altar when something better comes along. So is it fair or ethical that they may string you along? Not really, but when you see it from their point of view, you can understand the dance a little better.

Here's something else to watch out for. Coaches may be genuinely interested at the time of a campus visit that happens late in junior year or during the summer between junior and senior years. Fall of senior year comes, your kid applies to the school, and you all think you've got it in the bag. Then during senior year, they become less impressed with your kid or someone else comes along that steals their heart. You have no way of knowing. Some coaches will spell it out, others will not. Some student-athletes/parents will hear a coach's lack of enthusiasm, others will not. Let's say your kid is accepted to the school and decides to go there, not realizing someone has taken their spot. Only after they show up on campus does it become clear that this is not going to be your child's dream situation.

So how do you protect yourself?

First, be honest with yourself about what answer you get when you ask that question. Hear what they really say, not just what you want to hear.

Students and parents hear what they want to hear. I have coached at OWU for thirty-one years and I have never told a young man he could start or even play at OWU, yet many hear that they can play/start.

Jay Martin, Head Coach, Men's Soccer, Ohio Wesleyan University

---

A common misunderstanding is confusion over what a coach says and what parents hear.

Timothy Shea, Head Coach, Women's Basketball, Salem State College

---

Ask for clarification if you don't understand. And trust your gut instincts. You've been down this road before in dating relationships, and you know when you're being strung along.

Second, make sure you have several schools that like you, that you like and are willing to play for, and that you apply to. If you limit yourself to only the one school that's at the top of your list, you are setting yourself up for disappointment and disaster if it doesn't come through for you. You may find yourself getting rejected by the admissions office at the eleventh hour or told you will have to resort to walk-on status.

Here is a list of good, hard questions for the coaching staff:

- ✧ **How many athletes are you recruiting for my position?**
- ✧ **Where am I on the depth chart?**
- ✧ **What are my chances of playing as a freshman?** (Supplement this by asking, **how often do you play freshmen?** Your chances of playing as a freshman will depend very much on your performance, attitude, etc., and the coach won't know that at this point. But whether or not they are inclined to play freshmen is a question that can be answered by looking at a few years of history.)

- **What are my chances of ever being a starter?** When they say something like, that depends on how hard you work—blah blah blah, you ask, **if you had to make the decision today based on what you know about me right now and what you know about the other players currently on the team and those you are recruiting, how would you answer that?**

- **What is the likelihood that I will gain admission to the school?** They will say that they don't make admissions decisions, only the admissions office does. This is true, but you're not asking for guarantees here, just the likelihood. So next ask, **based on your past experience with kids you wanted for this program, how do my credentials compare with those who have and haven't gained admission?**

- **What would your players tell me they like most and least about you?** Of course you will ask the players this as well, but it's always interesting to hear it from the coach's point of view.

- **What makes your school and program so good? How does it stand out from others?**

Compatibility with the Coach

Before we move on, let's consider what you need to know about the coach. First and foremost, there are no coaching guarantees. Obviously, you should avoid a program where you have conflicts with the coach. But if you pick a program strictly on the basis of liking the coach, you could be unhappy if the coach leaves. It's more common than it should be, and unless you have insider information, you won't have any way of knowing beforehand.

THE INSIDE TRACK

Fall in love with a school and a sports program, not a coach. The school and program won't ever leave you.

You should never base your decision on the coach alone as we tend to move every four to five years, but we are the people who have the most contact with the student-athlete outside of their parents. Such is the dilemma, but the coach reflects the demeanor and attitude of the team and program and has to be a major consideration.

Steven Keith, Head Coach, Cross Country, Vanderbilt University

Curveball

Remember Mike, the football player who ended up as a preferred walk-on? The coach wanted him but wasn't in a position to offer him a scholarship. Without a commitment, Mike had to earn his chance to play. One of the appealing things about being a preferred walk-on at this school was that the coach who recruited him had a history of saving two of his scholarships every year for upperclassmen that were preferred walk-ons. He used this to motivate and reward them for their efforts and commitment to his program. By the time Mike enrolled, this coach was gone. It remains to be seen if the new coach will continue this practice. ■

Despite the lack of guarantees, it's still in your child's best interest to understand as much about the current coaching staff as possible as this group of people will have a tremendous impact on your child's life over the next four years. Missy, the volleyball player, might have ended up playing all four years if she had been a little more careful about understanding her coach's style and how it conflicted with hers. Did you notice the reference to the coaching staff, not just the (head) coach? Your child may have a lot more day-to-day contact with the assistants than the head coach, and they will probably have a great deal of influence on your child's satisfaction with the program. If there's anyone on the staff that makes your child uncomfortable, take it as a red flag. There are several ways you can find out about the coaching staff:

- ◇ As mentioned beforehand, ask the coaches what their players would say about them.

- ◇ Talk to the other team members during your campus visit; they will tell you the truth.

- ◇ Observe a team practice.

- ◇ Watch the team compete.

- ◇ Read the coaches' bios on the school's website.

- ◇ Look at the head coaches coaching history—do they move around often?

- ◇ Ask the head coach for the names of some players who have graduated or have played for them at previous schools and call them for a reference. Would you have surgery done without checking references for the doctor? Would you hire someone for a job without checking references from their past jobs? You're not looking for skeletons in the closet here, just indications that this person's style is compatible with yours.

To assume that all college coaches, by definition, are better than coaches you've had in club or high school soccer is just not a good idea. In fact, there are good and bad, honest and unethical, conscientious and careless coaches at every level, in every corner of the U.S..

Brian Parker, Head Coach, Women's Soccer, Frostburg State University

---

Closing thoughts on how coaches communicate

One last thing to consider about the communication between you and the different coaches you are being recruited by is that they all have different processes and styles. You have to be careful not to compare them and come to the conclusion that one is more interested than another because they have different styles of recruiting. Again, the message here is not to put all of your eggs in one basket, but protect yourself by going down this road with several programs that could be a good fit.

Recruiting in Division III is sometimes a numbers game, and as a coach, you don't always get a chance to show as much attention to all of your recruits even though you are interested in him.

Steven Mohr, Head Coach, Football, Trinity University

Coaches recruit differently. Some call every week—others do not. Take notice of the interest the coach has in you when you visit...eye-to-eye contact is the best way to learn more about a coach...not by lengthy e-mails or phone calls every week talking about the weather.

George Kennedy, Head Coach, Swim and Dive, Johns Hopkins University

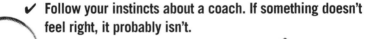

·KEEPING SCORE·

- ✔ Encourage your child to use the Internet to learn more about the schools that are contacting them.
- ✔ Coax your child to diplomatically cut loose the schools they're not interested in.
- ✔ Have your child put together a good list of coach questions by using those in this chapter and any of your own. Make copies and encourage your kid to keep it by the phone and take it on campus visits.
- ✔ Follow your instincts about a coach. If something doesn't feel right, it probably isn't.

CHAPTER 14

THE CAMPUS VISIT

What Exactly Happens on the Campus Visit?

As with the last chapter, this chapter should be read by your student-athlete. In the earliest stages of your search, you will want to visit a range of campus types to get a sense of what feels right. Pick large and small, rural, urban, and suburban. Other than taking the cursory campus tour, these first visits are just to acclimate your child to what the search process is like. As a result, you may be able to rule out some schools on your list.

Once you focus in on the set of schools you're seriously considering and you've got mutual interest from the coaches there, the sport-focused official or unofficial campus visit provides you with a great opportunity. Hopefully you will have about six schools on your list at this point in time. You will get a much fuller view of what life will be like for you there than most of your non-athletic friends will on their campus visits. You will do all of the things that your friends are doing—tour the campus, go to an information session, possibly go to a class or meet with someone in your academic area of interest. But you will also meet the coaching staff and tour the athletic facilities. You will probably eat lunch with the coach or some of the team, and depending on what time of year you're there, you may be able to scrimmage with the team or watch them practice. As a student-athlete, you will get to stay overnight in the dorms with one of the players, and you will probably socialize with other team members. Since these are the people you will be hanging out with more than anyone else, you need to know your comfort level with this group. By the time you leave, you will have a good idea if this is a place that is a perfect fit, an okay fit, or not a fit. And keep in mind that you are not the only one thinking and evaluating. There is another reason the coaches want you to spend the night in the dorm with the players…so read on.

Judgment in the Court of Common Sense

It is foolish to think the judging is over when the coach leaves the room. As one coach told us, **leave a kid with the team members and their true colors will eventually come out.** Every coach knows that a kid is going to be on their best behavior in front of the coaching staff. But the team members have even more to lose from a poor choice—they have to like being around your child, they have to feel like your kid will have the greater good as their first priority, can help them win, and has respect for their experience.

Everyone is judging you, not just the coaching staff.

Be prepared for the team members to put your child in new and potentially uncomfortable situations. They may take him or her out drinking. It's what some of them do themselves, and it makes the recruit feel "grown up." Have a conversation before the visits about this possibility and talk through approaches your child can take in this situation. You will want to take control, but the reality is that you will not be there and won't even know it's happening, so your kid will have to make some decisions. Knowing this might happen gives kids the opportunity to think through how to handle it so they won't do something they'll regret later, as illustrated below.

You're Always On

Three recruits were on an overnight campus visit. They joined the basketball team for an informal workout and later that evening went with some of the guys to a student's birthday party. One of the recruits drank pretty heavily. Some of the upperclassman on the team started teasing him, encouraging him to do silly stunts. While this was going on, they were telling the other two recruits that this kid was making an idiot of himself. He thought he was fitting in whereas they really were making fun of him. He was not recruited beyond that night. ■

You should also be aware of how you are presenting yourself if you practice or scrimmage with the current team members. This might not happen if you participate in a solo sport like swimming or track, because your times will provide enough information to evaluate you with, but if you participate in a team sport, you may have the opportunity to work out or informally practice with the team. In a scrimmage, it's all about being a team-oriented player. They don't want you to be a doormat, but at the same time, they don't want you to feel the need to prove yourself. If you've got skills, it will come out. There is nothing more offensive than when someone tries to showcase and upstage the team. Remember, you're being judged every step of the way, and the team members may be even tougher on you than the coaching staff. Don't let the fact that they are your contemporaries blind you to this; they can vote you off the island pretty quickly.

Thoughts about the campus tour

Most of the time, a student who doesn't know (or care) that your kid is a student-athlete will lead the campus tour. If you're lucky, one of the coaches will take you on a personal tour, showing your kid the things that are most important for them to see. Otherwise, the normal tour route is through the admissions office and the general tours that are offered to everyone visiting the campus. The problem with these general tours is that **kids will assume that every student on that campus is just like their tour guide**. They don't do this because they're stupid—they do it because the whole college choice process is so overwhelming that they look to any small piece of information to help them narrow down their choices, so they generalize about campus personality and campus culture in any way they can. Ever hear a story about a kid loving a campus because the weather was beautiful or hating a campus because it was raining and dreary? It's only a two-hour snapshot, but it creates an impression upon which they can make a decision. Your objective is to reduce the chance of rejecting a school for the wrong reason.

After the kids and parents gather at the admissions office, a group of student volunteers will magically appear. At some campuses, they will assign you to the group and you will be powerless to influence it. At others, they just ask the group to split up so that roughly ten to fifteen end up with each tour guide and away you go. If you are given the choice, scan the available students and hook up with the one who looks most like someone your kid can relate to and feel comfortable with. Too many kids will be turned off to a school because their impression of the school is based on one kid they can't connect with, and they won't see that there are plenty of other normal kids on campus. They will have four years to become more broad-minded. It doesn't have to happen on this day.

Fortunately for you, if your kid feels really comfortable with the other students/team members they meet, they may not place so much emphasis on generalizing about the student body from this one tour guide. Conversely, if the student body seems fine but your kid doesn't feel like s/he fits with the team, game over. Another strategy might be to ask the coaching staff if one of the team members can take your child on the informal walk-around. They won't be "trained" as thoroughly as the tour guides, but the benefits will outweigh their potential lack of knowledge of campus geography.

When Should You Visit the Campus?

The short answer is that you should visit some time before your child's senior year sport season, and you should try to have all of your visits done by the end of the fall. That doesn't mean wait until your senior year—junior year visits are preferable because you will have time to return if you need another visit to decide—but don't wait any longer than the beginning of your sport season. Here are a few reasons why:

◆ You're always practicing or competing once the high school season starts and will find it almost impossible to carve out time for campus visits.

◆ If you go before your season (and presumably the college season) begins, you may be able to informally practice or scrimmage with the team members, and they will probably have more downtime to spend with you. Once they're "in season," you can observe a practice or game but you are not allowed to participate or be observed by the coaching staff, and as mentioned above, you will probably find it difficult to find the time for campus visits if you're "in season" as well. The worse case scenario is if you wait until the season is over, and there won't be anything to observe or participate in.

◆ If you put off all of your campus visits until the late winter or spring of senior year, you will have to apply to any school you may be considering so that you can make the application deadlines. That can be expensive and time consuming, and filling out applications is like pulling teeth for high school kids—particularly if they are schools you would have eliminated had you visited them earlier. If you've gotten the visits out of the way, you can eliminate the schools you're not interested in and focus your application efforts and money/fees on the ones that do interest you.

Don't wait on your visits. We have athletes every year that can't visit for weeks at a time because they now find themselves "in season."

Brian McLaughlin, Head Coach, Swimming and Diving, Montclair State University

So the visit schedule would be no later than junior year/summer before senior year for fall sports (swimming, soccer, golf, etc.), and fall of senior year for all other sports. The spring sports like baseball and track and field still benefit from fall visits because of the college application deadlines. But again, all hope is not lost if you're pushing toward spring of senior year and still making initial contacts with schools. If they're really interested, they may be able to make exceptions for a late application and it's always in your child's best interest to visit a school before making a final decision.

Questions to Ask

You need to go on these campus visits armed with a list of questions, and don't be shy about referring back to the list. Every college book and website has a list of general questions, so I won't repeat them here. At D-I and D-II schools, you can ask about finances, but at D-III schools, any conversations about financial aid and scholarships should happen with the financial aid office, not the coaching staff. This list is focused on what you need to know from the coaching staff and the team—aside from how to get money. Some of these questions may be repetitive with previous sections of this book. Use what makes sense to you and make sure your list reflects those things that are important to you.

For the Coaching Staff

✧ What position do you see me playing?

✧ How many freshman spots are you recruiting for?

✧ What other players are currently on the roster at that position?

✧ When do you think I can expect to play?

✧ How many other players are you currently recruiting for this position and where do I fit on the depth chart? (This is hard to ask but so important.)

✧ How many total players are on the roster and how many freshmen do you anticipate needing?

✧ What is your team's style of play/how do you run the team?

✧ How would you describe your coaching style?

✧ What has made someone successful on your team/what has made someone unsuccessful?

✧ What is the practice schedule in-season and out-of-season?

✧ What is the schedule for conditioning/weight training?

✧ What are the off-season requirements for summer and holiday breaks?

✧ Do you have a junior varsity and do all freshmen automatically play on the JV team?

✧ Do you automatically redshirt freshmen (i.e., make freshmen sit out for their first year and then they play the following four years)?

✧ What are the graduation rates for athletes on this team?

✧ What percent return to the team after freshman year?

✧ What is the travel schedule like?

✧ How much school will I miss?

✧ Are there academic tutors available?

✧ Does the team take any special trips (e.g., during the summer)?

✧ Will I be able to participate in a semester-abroad program?

✧ What are the living situations?

✧ Do the team players room together?

- ✧ Do the team players eat/study together?
- ✧ Do they all live in the same dorm?
- ✧ How long am I required to live on campus?
- ✧ When does the head coach's contract end and how long does he intend to stay?
- ✧ Is medical insurance required for my participation and does the school I provide it or do I?
- ✧ Who will be responsible for the medical expenses if I am seriously injured in team competition?
- ✧ What happens if I want to transfer to another school?
- ✧ How do you run your practices?

For the Current Team Members

- ✧ What's a typical day like?
- ✧ How do you like the coaching staff—how would you describe their style?
- ✧ Is it tough to keep up with your schoolwork?
- ✧ Is help (for schoolwork) accessible?
- ✧ How many hours per day do you need to work/study?
- ✧ How do the faculty and students treat athletes?
- ✧ How much of a fan base does the team have?
- ✧ How hard is the travel schedule?
- ✧ How much time do you devote to the team during season/off season?
- ✧ What do you like best/least about the sports program?
- ✧ How are the living arrangements?
- ✧ Do the team players hang out together or do they go their own ways?
- ✧ What is there to do socially and how much time do you have for socializing?
- ✧ If you had to do it over again, would you still choose this school? Why/why not?

Highlight on One Important Question: When Can I Expect to Play?

Every player wants to know the answer to this, and of course you have a right to ask. Occasionally, a coach may even be able to honestly tell your child the words you want to hear (we need you right away, you will start as a freshman) because there are always circumstances where s/he is desperately undermanned in your child's position, and they know your child will be able to play right away. But before you limit yourself to only considering programs where you get a promise to play right away, I want to give you another perspective on this issue.

As mentioned before, many of you will come to collegiate recruiting after years and years (translation: many dollars spent) of club, AAU, and travel teams. Given the investment, many parents are sorely disappointed when this doesn't result in a scholarship. As discussed previously, participation in club sports only guarantees that your child will have the opportunity for continued development and exposure, *but they must take it from there. It's your child's skills, motivation, work ethic, sportsmanship, and willingness to do whatever it takes to improve that will earn him or her whatever s/he gets next.* Participating in club sports just opens the door; only your child is in control of the steps they take when they walk through it.

For some people, collegiate athletic recruiting is subject to these same notions of money in/promise out. Particularly for parents who have to pay some or all of their child's college expenses, there can be an assumption that their investment should at least garner the promise of playing time. Wrong again. Your investment is purchasing your child *an education*; the playing time must be earned each and every day by your child's efforts. Assuming that paying (at least partially) to attend a school should guarantee you playing time is like sending your child to a college where they party all the time, cut classes and fail, but still expect a degree.

A coach should be telling you something similar to what we heard when we were on the recruiting trail: based on what they know about you, you have great potential to be an impact player in this program, but that you will have to work hard to get (and keep) your playing time, and that the other players will be advised to do the same.

A common misunderstanding is, "my kid will start as a freshman, they really want him." Only a player's performance in practice and in games will EARN him a starting role!

Rich Lackner, Head Coach, Football, Carnegie Mellon University

---

I don't see this in track but I see this in my colleague's sports. Parents feel that since they are paying for the kid to go to school, then the athlete "deserves" or is "entitled" to the right to play. It should be a basic premise that you need to earn your right to play but that unfortunately is the problem. Some people see athletics as a "right" instead of a privilege. Students have a right to have the opportunity to participate, but they do not have the right to make a team, nor do they have the right to play or have playing time.

Dr. Toby C. Schwarz, Head Coach, Track and Field and Cross Country, Whitworth University

---

Following are some questions that wouldn't be asked of anyone directly, but your child needs to ponder them to see how important they are to him or her.

- ◇ Past track record of the team (Consistent winners? Up and down?).
- ◇ Do you want the opportunity to help a team rebuild or would you rather walk into a well-oiled machine?
- ◇ Conference they play in.
- ◇ Chances of getting to post-season play.
- ◇ The athletic facilities available—are they big enough/new enough/are they maintained well?
- ◇ Impressions about the coach and players—how well you fit.
- ◇ Stability of the coaching—will this coach be around for your four years?
- ◇ How do you view a younger, less experienced coach vs. an older and more experienced coach?
- ◇ Philosophy of the athletic director. If the coach leaves, it will be the AD's job to hire the next coach. Do you agree with the AD in philosophy?
- ◇ Do they play a similar style to what you're best suited for?
- ◇ How important is student support/fan support?

·KEEPING SCORE·

✔ When you get a letter with a questionnaire, fill it out and send it back promptly. It doesn't commit you to anything, but not sending it back sends a message of disinterest and complacency.

✔ Send out your mailing to any new schools that have contacted you and look interesting.

✔ Set up your campus visits, paying close attention to the timing suggested in this book.

✔ Have a discussion with your child about how they should handle any awkward situations that may arise during their campus visit.

✔ Generate your list of questions for the coaching staff and players.

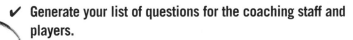

PART FIVE

Making the Decision

CHAPTER 15

DECIDING WHICH OFFER IS BEST

Between D-I or II and D-III

L et's assume your child has more than one school interested, and they span across both Division III and Division I or II. The D-I/D-II offer is likely to be a scholarship offer, but it won't necessarily be a full scholarship, particularly for D-II. It will probably come in the fall of senior year. The D-III offer won't include an athletic scholarship and it won't be a real "offer" because there are no binding commitments in D-III. It will be more of an expression of serious interest and the D-III school could sweeten the pot by offering some combination of merit scholarship and need-based financial aid. One of the challenges is that you may be asked to sign a commitment letter for a D-I/D-II program in the fall, before you have full information about the financial offer coming from a D-III school. If the D-I/D-II offer is a full scholarship, you probably won't care what the D-III offer is, but if it's a partial scholarship, the comparison gets a little closer.

THE INSIDE TRACK

Many scholarship offers have a short time fuse. Turn it down and it goes to the next one on the list. Don't assume it will still be there if you refuse and then change your mind.

Here are some thoughts from D-I coaches on the differences between expectations of D-I and D-III players:

The time commitment

The biggest difference seems to be the time commitment and the potential impact it has on academic focus. D-I schools allow year-round involvement and there are specific NCAA guidelines that D-I schools must follow: no more than twenty hours per week in season and eight hours per week out of season. (There is more to the guidelines but this is sufficient for our purposes.) D-III programs cannot have out-of-season training programs. This means that as a D-I athlete, you basically have a year-round job that includes summers and the off-season part of the school year. As a D-III athlete, your summers and your out-of-season training during the school year are governed by your own motivation and the culture/expectations of the other team members, but not by required elements of the program. Keep in mind that the increased time commitments expected of D-I athletes are expected for both scholarship and non-scholarship kids. This may impact how you compare a non-scholarship offer from a D-I school with a D-III school.

You put a lot more time in at a scholarship school. The student-athletes are usually being compensated with a scholarship and thus are sometimes treated like employees. Weight workouts are required, running workouts are required, etc. I know they "require" them at D-III schools, but it's different. There are fewer excuses for missing things because we pay for school. There are fewer class conflicts during practice time at a D-I school because we can dictate when the players can take the classes that we are paying for.

Roc Bellantoni, Assistant Head Coach, Football, Eastern Illinois University

The difference is in the amount of time devoted to sport. Travel, practice, study hall, etc. They miss more class and it is more of a job at the D-I level.

Krista Kilburn-Steveskey, Head Coach, Women's Basketball, Hofstra University

But at the same time, D-I schools recognize the time burden they are putting on athletes and offer more extensive academic services to student-athletes than D-III schools do.

The support system in D-I is much better via academic counseling—tutors, study hall, assisted registration, etc.

Diane Drake, Head Coach, Women's Soccer, George Mason University

What about athletic ability differences

Coaches' views about differences in athletic ability between D-I players and D-III players vary. Some view all D-I athletes as bigger, stronger, and faster, regardless of sport. Others think there are many equally talented athletes in D-III programs who have chosen them for personal reasons. Regardless of division, the coach and the program will have high expectations of any student-athlete.

My expectations are the same for our players (walk-on and scholarship) that I would have at a D-III: compete to the best of your ability on the court and in the classroom, and represent your teammates and university the right way with your actions.

Brad Stevens, Head Coach Men's Basketball, Butler University

D-III is a very competitive world in athletics; don't fool yourself.

Steven Keith, Head Coach, Cross Country, Vanderbilt University

Other considerations

Depending on your sport, the D-I competition may have television coverage and will be more likely to get national media coverage of some kind. Competition will probably also include larger crowds and more fan support. D-III competition rarely gets media coverage, and crowd sizes and fan support will vary from school to school.

A low D-I/high D-III athlete will probably be more of an impact player at the D-III level with less time commitment. This is the "big fish in a small pond vs. small fish in a big pond" idea. I recently read an interview with a D-III athlete during his senior year at Washington University in St. Louis as his athletic career was winding down. When he made his college decision four years earlier, he had turned down several D-I offers. What he said was reflective of this "big fish in a small pond" notion. Most of the D-I schools he was looking at played at the bottom of their conference and the ones that were somewhat competitive still had no chance at a national title. They were also mostly mediocre academic schools. He chose a strong sports program at a strong academic D-III school, got into the final four as a junior, won the national championship as a senior, and won virtually every D-III award possible. He plans to go on to graduate school. Sounds like his choice worked out well for him.

Summary of D-I vs. D-III Decision

There is no doubt that the financial burden of a college education is minimized with a scholarship offer, but you must keep in mind that when a student-athlete accepts a scholarship, s/he effectively becomes an employee of that university. The school can make decisions on a variety of issues and you and your child may not be willing to give up decision-making control over all of them. Some of these decisions are:

- ✧ What classes they can take
- ✧ When they can take their classes
- ✧ How many hours they can carry each semester
- ✧ If they have to attend summer school
- ✧ The type of outside activities they can become involved in
- ✧ When they have to study
- ✧ When they can go home for vacations
- ✧ How much time they need to spend in sport-related activities

Between Public and Private Schools

What if your child has interest from both public and private universities? There are some differences to consider. Public schools tend to have many more general programs but more limited resources that are governed by that state's legislature. Retention is not the main criteria they are measured by.

Private schools are more focused on retention and graduating all of their students. They may have much more specialized and distinguished programs in certain areas and, conversely, have much less to offer in other areas. For example, many of the smaller, private liberal arts colleges don't offer a degree program in business. Because they are privately funded, they can commit (or withdraw) their resources to anything they want to, including their athletic programs. Again, just make sure you fully understand the scope and the mission of the schools looking at your child.

Between Schools within D-III

Suppose your child has several D-III schools competing for them. Chances are, some of them are completely new to you and you've been scrambling to try to learn about them academically, financially, athletically, geographically, and so on. How do you compare? One suggestion is to try to put some numbers around your child's priorities. The following list will give you several of the characteristics to consider. Most have appeared previously in the college selection sections.

First, have your child prioritize the schools in terms of which is the most important to the least important. In the worksheet example at the end of this chapter, the most important is ranked highest (10) and the least important is ranked lowest (1).

Then list your potential schools across the top and give each school a rating from 1-5 on how well it meets or satisfies each criterion. In this example, we compare three D-III schools. The better the school met the criteria, the higher the rating (5). If the school didn't meet the criteria at all, it was given a 1.

Now, multiply the ratings by the rankings, add them up, and see how the schools stack up. Each school will end up with a total score. This is not intended to be a mathematical solution to your decision, but it will give you an idea of which schools should be in the consideration set and which should drop out.

Here's a list to start with. The worksheet example considers ten of these. Add and subtract criteria according to what's important to you.

Price tag	Location type (rural/urban/suburban/etc.)
Size of student population	Quality of intended program of study
Distance from home	Sense of "fit" with the kids on campus
Weather	Chances of getting to postseason
Access to a city	Team's past record
Financial offer	Access to high school friends
Quality of academics	Conference they compete in
Fit with team style of play	Overall time commitment to your sport
How quickly will you play	Fit with the team members
Likelihood of being an impact player	Like the coaching staff
Size and enthusiasm of fan base	

The following is a worksheet example for comparing three schools on ten of these criteria:

	Importance*	Scl-1	total	Scl-2	total	Scl-3	Total
Distance from home	9	5	45	1	9	4	36
Setting***	8	2	16	3	24	5	40
City access	3	1	3	1	3	5	15
Scholarship $$ offered	7	4	28	2	14	1	7
Quality of academics	1	4	4	4	4	5	5
Fit with sports team members**	10	4	40	5	50	5	50
Like coaches	4	5	20	5	20	5	20
Fit with team style of play**	6	4	24	5	30	4	24
Likelihood of being impact player	5	5	25	5	25	4	20
Chances of postseason	2	2	<u>4</u>	3	<u>6</u>	5	<u>10</u>
Totals			209		185		227

*higher number = more important ** scale of 1-5 where 5 = good fit
*** setting = rural, urban, suburban

Steps to Create Your Worksheet

Step 1: Rank how important each criterion is—most important is highest number, least is lowest number.

Step 2: Rate how well each school meets that criteria. If the school meets it perfectly, rate it a 5. If the school doesn't meet it, rate it a 1. (Example: student wants access to a city. School 1 is very rural so it receives a 1, but school 3 is in a city so it receives a 5.)

Step 3: Multiply the rank by each school's rating for that school's total.

Step 4: Add up the total across all criteria for each school. In this example, school 3 is the best fit for this student.

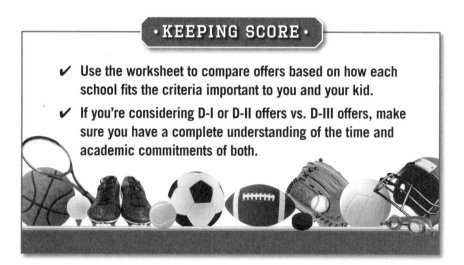

· KEEPING SCORE ·

✔ Use the worksheet to compare offers based on how each school fits the criteria important to you and your kid.

✔ If you're considering D-I or D-II offers vs. D-III offers, make sure you have a complete understanding of the time and academic commitments of both.

16

WHEN DO YOU MAKE THE FINAL DECISION?

The timing of your decision will most likely be contingent on whether or not there is a scholarship involved. Most scholarship offers are not open-ended, and coaches will often ask for the decision to be made within a timeframe that allows them to offer to someone else if your child turns it down. If there is not a scholarship involved, decisions are typically made later because there is no commitment involved that would drive an earlier decision, and some student-athletes wait until the last minute to see if a scholarship will materialize. Following is some more detailed information about the timing options.

If There Is a Scholarship

If you're being offered a D-I or D-II scholarship, the vast majority of these priority-recruiting decisions are made close to November of senior year, and these students are asked to sign a "national letter of intent" indicating their commitment to this particular school. You can find information about it at www.national-letter.org. Both parties benefit from this practice. For the institution, it commits an athlete to fill an available spot so they can stop recruiting for that spot. For the student-athlete, it ensures one year of either partial or full financial aid, and it calls off the dogs so no one else can officially recruit the student. By completing this process in the fall of senior year, the heavily recruited student-athlete can relax a little and be freed from constant recruiting pressure (a problem I'm sure most of your kids would love to have). Here are a few important things to know about the national letter of intent—the rest you can find on the website:

First and foremost, the national letter of intent represents a commitment on the part of both parties and *there are repercussions for breaking this commitment.* The penalty for breaking the commitment to a school once your child has signed is the loss of a full year of eligibility, and your kid will have to be a resident on the campus of the next school they sign with for a full year before participating in a sport. Understand that the agreement is between the student and the school, not the student and the coach. If your child has chosen this school because of the coach and the coach leaves, your kid is out of luck.

Every sport has specific signing times and most are in November, but there are some variations to the timing, most notably football, which has a signing date in February.

There are about five hundred schools that participate in the national letter of intent program: most D-I and D-II schools participate. The schools that don't participate are the service academies, the Ivy League, some Patriot League schools, D-III, NAIA, prep schools, junior colleges, and community colleges.

Ivy League schools don't participate because they don't offer athletic scholarships. Instead, they may send out what's called a "likely letter," which essentially guarantees admission to a candidate prior to official admissions decisions coming out. The reason they do this is that these candidates may have to make decisions about scholarship offers from other schools before they would have an official admissions offer from an Ivy League school. This assures student-athletes who choose Ivy League schools over scholarship offers from other schools that they will gain admissions, so they can turn down scholarship offers.

The timing of scholarship offers and decisions means that if your child falls into one of these categories, *all of your research and visits will need to be completed by fall of senior year.* If not, you may find yourself scrambling to react to the handful of schools that are pursuing you and missing out on others you might have been interested in.

Having said all this about fall timing, note that there are still scholarships offered later in the year as not every school will fill every position they're recruiting for according to this timing. Transfers also will leave scholarship openings that can still be filled late in the year.

If There Is Not a Scholarship

The landscape for timing is different if your child doesn't have a scholarship offer because without one, there is really no such thing as a commitment. A coach may pursue your child with great enthusiasm and your child may profess a strong preference for a particular program, but in the end, either party can choose to go elsewhere with no repercussions. The only thing that comes close to resembling a commitment at a D-III institution is an early decision application, and it has both benefits and drawbacks for the student. Deciding between early decision and regular decision is also relevant for non-recruited athletes who hope to be walk-ons at a D-I or D-II program.

If you fall into one of these categories for which early vs. regular decision is relevant, pay attention as you're looking at different schools to how their application and admissions processes works. Some schools have rolling admissions. The earlier you apply, the earlier you will have a decision. These schools clearly keep making admissions decisions until all of their slots are filled. Schools that have more traditional options force you to make some choices. You will see early decision, early action, and regular decision. Regardless of which route you choose, make sure you know the various deadlines for applications to admissions and financial aid. It's always in your best interest to apply as early as possible. There are three reasons for this:

1. The more selective the school, the less flexibility a coach has with these deadlines.

2. Admissions personnel face a crunch in applications as soon as the deadline for their school passes, and it may be to your advantage to not get caught in that crunch.

3. Some financial aid programs have less to work with as they get deeper into the admissions process.

So how exactly does early decision work?

Early decision means that you apply by an early deadline, you find out if you're accepted early, and if you are, *it is a binding commitment, so you must go to that school.* But understand that the commitment part of this only applies to your child having to attend the school.

THE INSIDE TRACK

An early decision acceptance means you're accepted to the school, not the sports program. Your child is not obligated to participate in the sports program, and just as important, the coach is not obligated to give them a spot on the team.

For that matter, a D-I signing only commits the school to provide a year of financial aid to student-athletes, not to give them any playing time. It's hard to imagine why a coach would waste a scholarship on someone they don't want to develop and play—that's why it's a pretty solid commitment. The early decision commitment at a D-III school tells a coach that your child will attend if they get in, and that no one else can recruit them. That's a pretty strong message to a coach that your child means business. Coaches who have any ethical integrity at all should discourage kids from applying early decision if they know that there's no role for them on the team.

You can only apply to one school as an early decision candidate and you must withdraw your applications to other schools if you are accepted.

The reason that it affects the timing of your decision is because the timeframe is typically as follows: applications are due in November, and admission decisions are mailed out in December—both several months earlier than normal admissions deadlines. Some schools have a second early decision deadline that is the same as the regular decision deadline for applications (for example, January 15), but you will get your decision within a month.

Early decision is a good option if:

> ✧ **Your child knows unequivocally that they want to attend that school.**
>
> ✧ **Your child wants the college choice behind them so they can relax and enjoy the rest of their senior year.**
>
> ✧ **Your child wants to "secure" a spot on that team that others may be in consideration for as well (see the next page for a fuller description of this situation). While you probably won't know how vulnerable the spot is, better to be the scooper instead of the kid who got scooped.**

Some research indicates higher acceptance rates for early admissions candidates than regular admissions candidates. The coach may have more clout with admissions to gain acceptance for early decision candidates, particularly in schools with highly competitive academic standards. Remember, everyone is more inclined to like people who clearly like them.

Early decision can increase the chances of getting in but there are no guarantees.

Matt Smith, Head Coach, Men's Soccer, Johns Hopkins University

However, there are two important downsides to early decision that you need to be aware of:

1. Early decision favors students from families with less financial constraints because you won't know what need-based or merit-based scholarship money will be available to you at the time of your application. Because it's a binding commitment, you need to understand what your options are. If you apply for need-based financial aid, you will typically find out how much you are getting shortly after you get your acceptance letter and you do have the right to withdraw your application (i.e., be released from the binding commitment) if you feel that it's not enough. But if you are depending on getting some merit-based scholarship money for your child to attend this program, you won't know how much, if any, merit-based money your child is going to receive until much later, and your child will be committed to attending this school. If

you don't receive the merit aid you were counting on, you're in trouble. Or if you need to compare the financial aid packages offered by several schools before you make a final decision, you will need to wait until you receive all of them. That will effectively take you out of the early decision pool. If the final choice of school can't be made without a full understanding of how the options stack up financially, early decision is not for you. In fact, some schools are doing away with early decision as an option because they feel that it "disadvantages the disadvantaged" by giving the edge to more economically privileged students who don't need to wait for the spring to compare financial aid offers. As of fall of 2008, Harvard, Princeton, and the University of Virginia all dropped their early admissions programs.

2. And very important, because it's a binding commitment, you cannot consider any other options that might come your way. If your child has an eye on other schools and would regret this choice if those other schools got interested later in the year, early decision is not for you. But if your child is pretty confident that this school and athletic program are ideal, there is great relief in having the decision behind him or her. Further, if your kid doesn't gain acceptance into the school of his or her dreams, there is still plenty of time to explore other options.

THE INSIDE TRACK

If your kid is a strong D-III candidate who is holding out for a D-I or D-II scholarship, stay away from early decision.

Early decision is great for coaches because it allows them to fill spots earlier and therefore have a better handle on exactly what their needs are as the year goes on. Perhaps even more important, if the highest priority recruits apply early decision, it lets the coach cut ties with the other kids they're talking to for that position, saving time and effort.

Early action is similar to early decision both in terms of timing for when the applications need to be in and when you will be notified, but it is not binding so you can still choose to go elsewhere. This is a great situation because it gives your child all the benefits of early decision without the negatives of the lack of financial aid information prior to the final decision and without taking away any of their other options. If your child has a clear frontrunner that offers early action, it's a no-brainer.

In comparison, *regular decisions* have the latest due dates for applications and decisions are usually rendered in April.

If early decision is too limiting in terms of knowing the financial package and shutting down other options, why not just apply everywhere with a regular decision status?

First, as mentioned above, lots of kids don't want to spend most of their senior year wondering where they will attend school and if they'll get in. This is a weight on their shoulders that will gain pounds as the year goes on, and regular decisions aren't sent out until early April. If it doesn't go as planned, it's pretty late to do anything about it.

Another subtle benefit of early decision is that your child has time to develop a relationship with future teammates and the coaching staff. The college team is going to be in-season at the same time the high school student is and they can track each other's seasons. They will both feel more comfortable with each other when your child's freshman year begins.

Now, back to getting scooped. Please share this scenario with your child so they will understand how it can play out. This has to do with hedging your bets about who else is available to a coach at a given school, particularly one your child is very interested in. Let's go back to the notion of four or five people that the coach is looking at for each open spot. Let's say the coach has met all five kids who are vying for your position and really likes three of the five and would be comfortable with any of them. Let's assume that you know you're one of those top three. You like this program a lot and let the coach know that you're going to apply—regular decision. But of course, a regular decision application doesn't guarantee the coach that you'll come there if you gain admission, just that the school is in your consideration set. So your application does nothing to help define this coach's next recruiting class until April/May when you have to make your decision. Unbeknownst to you, another one of the three is applying early decision. The coach knows that if this kid gains admission, he's got a definite addition to his program since it's binding. He also knows he will have a definite answer several months earlier, and chances are, the coach will run this kid's application through the admissions office to check for red flags so they will probably have a pretty good

177

idea of this kid's status very quickly. While you're busy thinking this school is one that is interested in you, they suddenly stop communicating with you, or they call and cut you loose. Mr./Ms. Early Decision just scooped you and took the spot that could have gone to either of you. That's the calculated risk of hanging back. That doesn't mean you can't apply to the school, and you can still go out for the team if you gain admission, but if the coach has stopped calling and has let your child know they already have someone for the spot your kid was hoping for, consider the writing to be on the wall.

Telling Coaches the Decision

In a perfect world, your child will have at least a few coaches interested, and will need to make a choice once they gain admission to the school(s). Whether your kid is a D-I scholarship athlete, a D-III non-scholarship athlete, an early decision candidate, or a regular decision candidate, s/he will have one easy call to make and that is to the coach who s/he has decided to play for. After the euphoria of this call, all recruited student-athletes have to inform the coaches at the schools they are not going to attend that they've made their decision and it doesn't include this coach's program. To give you a frame of reference for what this feels like to kids, remember back to when you got dragged to the doctor for a booster shot or to the dentist to get a cavity filled. Remember back to the first time you broke up with someone. This is a task that fills kids with dread, and they will try to put it off as long as humanly possible. I have suggestions for both of you.

For you, the parent

Be sympathetic and help your child craft exactly what to say to these coaches. Write it down if that helps. It will not come naturally or comfortably, and your support will make it a little easier.

This is something your child needs to do, don't offer to do it. The anticipation is always worse than the actual event, and the sun will still rise tomorrow.

Insist that this be done as a live phone conversation. No e-mails, text messages, or voice mails. These are people that have spent a fair amount of time and energy on your child and they are owed the respect of a real conversation. Remember that one of the reasons you are sending your child to college in the first place is so they can transition from childhood into adulthood. This is a teachable moment about the responsibilities of adulthood, so use it. Sermon over.

Also, from a practical point of view, ending the relationship on a positive note could help your child in the long run. Suppose the school choice they make just doesn't work out for some reason, and your child ends up wanting to transfer to another school. The school that was a second choice would be a likely starting point. The first thing your kid will want to know is if that coach is still interested and willing to take him or her in. It helps to have left a good impression.

For your child

Do it right away. There are several reasons for this. First, your dread will grow in proportion the longer you put it off. Second, these folks talk and word will spread quickly once a decision is made. You want them to hear it from you, not from another coach. Third, the quicker you let them know, the quicker they can extend an offer to someone else or adjust their planning. That should make you feel a little better.

When you give the other coaches your reasons for choosing the school that you did, focus on the things that were appealing about the choice you made, not what you didn't like about their school or their program. There is nothing to be gained by personalizing the rejection. Examples of reasons might be the size of the school, the type of setting, the proximity to home, and the amount of financial aid they offered—all criteria that are not a direct rejection of this coach and his program.

THE INSIDE TRACK

Coaches get rejections every year and not only do they expect it, but they over-recruit in anticipation of it.

Recognize that even though this is very difficult for you, it goes with the territory. The majority of coaches will be gracious, understanding, and will wish you the best of luck. If you run across a coach who doesn't respond this way, remember that they like to win (that's part of coaching) and just wish them the best of luck. They're adults. It's their problem and they'll get over it.

· KEEPING SCORE ·

✔ If you are considering signing a letter of intent for a scholarship offer, make sure you understand all the implications of this commitment.

✔ For each school on your list, know how their applications and admissions process works so you can leverage the timing in your favor.

✔ If you're considering D-III schools, weigh the pros and cons of early decision for your situation.

✔ Have your child make the calls to both the coach whose offer is being accepted, and the coaches who are being turned down. Role-play the conversation if you think it will help your child.

CHAPTER 17

CREATING A
BACKUP PLAN

H aving an alternative plan can't be overstressed. There are too many stories out there about kids who seemed to have built a great relationship with the coach/program they were most interested in, only to have it come crashing down when they couldn't secure the financial aid they needed, or the office of admissions weighed in with a negative. No matter how knowledgeable you are about the process, you can't guarantee this won't happen, so the only prudent course of action is to have a solid backup plan. Your backup plan should have a couple of parts to it.

If your child is absolutely set on *a specific school*

Research what other unique skills/talents that school may be looking for besides sports. For example, does your child have any talents or experience with singing, playing an instrument, art, debating, writing, and so on. Every school wants its student population to possess a wide range of talents and abilities, but no school expects each individual to possess them all. When you make your application to the school of your child's dreams, highlight every unique skill s/he has, not just the athletic ones. And s/he should still apply to several other schools.

If your child is absolutely set on *playing their sport*

Make sure you have found sports programs for your child at more than one school. Don't wait until you're blindsided with a rejection in April to start trying to figure out where else to go—it may be too late. Some schools may be able to still take you through the applications process after the deadlines, but not all are willing to do that. Develop and nurture relationships with several schools along the way. Remember, they're doing the same thing with several other student-athletes besides your child. Here is where having a good sense of how your kid stacks up to the competition becomes important. A "safety" school, in this context, is one at which your child would be a strong competitor athletically and would have the academic credentials to be a pretty sure bet for admission. It may not be a first choice, but there should be at least one school on the list that is clamoring for your child. And no attitude, please. Until the final decision is made (and the schools have made their decisions about your kid), your child needs to treat every school as though it would be a privilege to play for it.

If your child were looking at schools s/he wouldn't consider *without his sport*

Let's assume that one of several things happens between the time your child is considering their options, and the fall semester of college begins:

1. Your kid experiences career ending injury.

2. During senior year, your child is tired of committing so much to the sport and doesn't have the drive to keep playing in college (remember William Gates in the movie *Hoop Dreams*?).

3. Admission is denied to the schools that wanted your child to play the sport.

4. Your child is accepted but the coach makes it clear that there is no role on the team for your child.

Your backup plan needs to include applying to one or more schools that your child would have chosen *if playing their sport was never part of the landscape*. For example, if s/he would have attended a large public university with nationally prominent sports teams but are looking at smaller, private liberal arts schools because s/he wouldn't be competitive enough to play at a larger school, s/he should still apply there. In this context, a "safety" school is where s/he would choose if sports were out of the picture. It may be the same schools, but it may not. Just make sure to consider it.

In a D-I program, the pecking order is much clearer because of the scholarship. If they want you, they offer you at least a partial scholarship. No scholarship means less interest, and you'll have to take your chances as a walk-on if you really want to attend that school. As a D-III prospect who's not one of the coach's top choices but applies to the school anyway and gets in, you will have to be prepared to be on the team in a backup role. If you're okay with that, then it's a win/win for everyone. But if you're not, you have to have a backup plan.

In order to protect yourself in the event of an April rejection letter from your first-choice school, you must pursue several schools for your sport, and you must ask hard questions of the coaching staff to better understand where you are on the depth chart for your position.

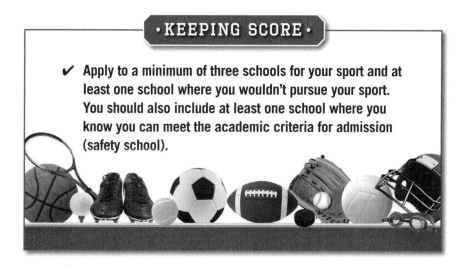

·KEEPING SCORE·

✔ Apply to a minimum of three schools for your sport and at least one school where you wouldn't pursue your sport. You should also include at least one school where you know you can meet the academic criteria for admission (safety school).

In Closing: A Happy Ending

Let me tell you how my story ended. My son narrowed his list to five schools and visited all of them in a four-week period in the early fall of his senior year. These were all schools that had been actively recruiting him so we knew he could potentially be successful at any of them. At each school, he was able to meet with the coaches and athletes, scrimmage with the team, and stay overnight in the dorms with a team member. At the end of four visits, the hit rate was pretty high. He took one off the list, was luke-warm on a second, and liked the other two a lot. He would have been happy going to either of them. The fifth visit was to a D-III school in St. Louis and it fit like Cinderella's slipper. As his father and I were busy going through the checklist (great academics—check, nice size—check, close enough to home—check, great basketball program—check, comfort with coach and players—check, access to a city—check), our son of few words needed only four to state his case: *what's not to like?* Game over. He chose to apply as an early decision candidate because he was sure of his choice, didn't want to take any chances, and wanted to enjoy playing high school ball his senior year without the added pressure of the college choice hanging over him. What followed was a great season of anticipation, looking forward to his first year playing college ball.

Now it's your turn. As my recruiting journey comes to an end, yours is just beginning, and I find myself a little envious. As exasperating as it can be, it is also one of the most exciting times in your child's life, and you get a front row seat on the rollercoaster. Would I do anything differently? Sure. Don't think for a minute that I followed all of my own advice. Hindsight is a great teacher, and I'm much smarter about this now than I was when I first dipped my toes into the recruiting waters. I'm encouraged to think that if you've read this book, you will probably benefit from what I've learned along the way. If I've done my job, you should be better informed and more confident about the process than I was when I was in your shoes. Armed with knowledge about recruiting, you've got everything you need to get going. It may feel like a big and onerous task. It is, but you only eat an elephant one bite at a time. Just get started and tackle a little piece each day.

It may be a pretty lonely experience. When you share your recruiting stories with friends whose kids aren't athletes, they will listen and acknowledge, but they won't really know what you're going through. When you share your stories with others going through the same thing, you will hold back a little, because you're not sure if they're having the same success and you don't want to make anyone else feel bad.

But despite the low odds that I spent much of this book sharing with you, there is no doubt in my mind that there is a collegiate athletic program for every kid that is reasonably skilled and has commitment, motivation, work ethic, and realistic expectations. You just have to put in the effort to find it and let them know your kid is out there. Good luck and get going—the perfect college is waiting to hear from you.

ACKNOWLEDGMENTS

My first dose of gratitude goes to all the people who shared their stories with me over the years. They unwittingly inspired me to find a way to infuse the world of hopeful student-athletes with a higher proportion of happy outcome stories and this book was the result.

To my early readers and reviewers, you shaped and molded what started as an intriguing possibility into something I am proud to share. Many thanks to Coach Pat Ambrose, Nancy Bateman, Wally Blazej, Cheryle Chamberlain, Coach Ken Davis, Lolly and Matt Dominski, Coach Mark Edwards, Bob Foltin, Andrea Friedlander, Ellen Grindel, Don Holton, Dave Rebnord, Jim Richter, Mary Robbins, Emily Selbe, and Carol Wicks. Andrea, you're a great critical thinker and your capacity for infinite drafts was a thing to behold. Emily, our shared passion for this always made me feel like you were right in the trenches with me. Dave, some of the best parts of this book were the result of your feedback.

A special thanks to Coach Pat Ambrose, Coach Mark Edwards, and Coach Ken Davis. Not only did you read every word and give me terrific feedback, your reactions convinced me that this book would add value to future student-athletes and their parents who would otherwise be way beyond my everyday reach.

Thanks to Melissa, Nancy, Diane, Jim and Amy, Wally, Emily, Andrea, Lolly and Matt, and Carol for allowing the stories of your kids to be examples that others can learn from.

Thanks to the dozens of college coaches who took the time to respond to my questions. You gave me such a broader perspective than I started with and your points of view are reflected in every part of this book. Athletic recruiting is clearly a topic you have thought long and hard about and are committed to improving.

To my project team, Emily Selbe, Peri Poloni-Gabriel, and Gail Kearns. You were a delight to work with. You respected my voice but polished it up beyond anything I could ever have imagined just a short time ago.

And finally, to my ever-supportive family. To my husband Jim—even though you were technically on the sidelines, you were a great asset. You always had obvious solutions when I got stuck, great words of encouragement when I faltered, and a direct path to the office copy machine on numerous occasions. Brady and Dylan, you patiently listened as I worked my way through, and interjected the fresh outlook of a generation that I can't pretend to be part of. And Dylan, thanks for giving me terrific material to create this book from. It was quite a journey.

APPENDIX A:
D-III CONFERENCES AND LINKS TO THEIR WEBSITES

Allegheny Mountain College Conference (AMCC)..................... www.amcconf.org

American Southwest Conference (ASC)......................... www.ascsports.org

Atlantic Central Football Conference (ACFC) .... www.acfcfootball.com

Capital Athletic Conference (CAC)............................. www.cacsports.com

Centennial Conference .... www.centennial.org

City University of New York Athletic Conference (CUNYAC) .... www.cunyathletics.com

College Conference of Illinois and Wisconsin (CCIW)..................... www.cciw.org

Commonwealth Coast Conference (CCC) .... www.thecommonwealthcoastconference.com

Empire Eight (E8) www.empire8.com

Great Northeast Athletic Conference (GNAC)..................... www.thegnac.com

Great South Athletic Conference (GSAC)....................... www.greatsouth.org

Heartland Collegiate Athletic Conference (HCAC) .... www.heartlandconf.org

Iowa Intercollegiate Athletic Conference (IIAC) .... www.iowaconference.com

Landmark Conference .... www.landmarkconference.org

Liberty League...................................... www.libertyleaguesports.org

Little East Conference...................................... www.littleeast.com

Massachusetts State College Athletic Conference (MASCAC) .... www.mascac.com

Michigan Intercollegiate Athletic Association (MIAA).................... www.miaa.org

Middle Atlantic States Collegiate Athletic Corporation................. www.mascac.org

Midwest Conference . . . . www.midwestconference.org

Minnesota Intercollegiate Athletic Conference (MIAC) . . . . www.miac-online.org

New England Collegiate Conference (NECC) . . . . www.neccathletics.com

New England Football Conference . . . . www.newenglandfootballconference.com

New England Small College Athletic Conference (NESCAC) . . . . www.nescac.com

New England Women's and Men's Athletic Conference (NEWMAC) . . www.newmaconline.com

New Jersey Athletic Conference . . . . www.njac.net

North Atlantic Conference (NAC) . . . . www.nacathletics.com

North Coast Athletic Conference (NCAC) . . . . www.northcoast.org

North Eastern Athletic Conference . . . . www.neacsports.com

Northern Athletics Conference . . . . www.northernathleticsconf.com

Northwest Conference . . . . www.northwestconference.net

Ohio Athletic Conference (OAC) . . . . www.oac.org

Old Dominion Athletic Conference (ODAC) . . . . www.odaconline.com

Pennsylvania Athletic Conference . . . . www.thepaconline.org

President's Athletic Conference (PAC) . . . . www.pacathletics.org

Skyline Conference . . . . www.skylineconference.org

SoCal Intercollegiate Athletic Conference (SCIAC) . . . . www.thesciac.org

Southern Collegiate Athletic Conference (SCAC) . . . . www.scac-online.org

St. Louis Intercollegiate Athletic Conference (SLIAC) . . . . www.sliac.org

State U of New York Athletic Conference (SUNYAC) . . . . www.sunyac.com

Upper Midwest Athletic Conference (UMAC) . . . . www.umacathletics.com

University Athletic Association (UAA) . . . . www.uaa.rochester.edu

USA South Atlantic Conference . . . . www.usasouth.net

Wisconsin Intercollegiate Athletic Conference (WIAC) . . . . www.uwsa.edu/wiac/

2008 NCAA BASKETBALL ATTENDANCE

Division I Men's Basketball Attendance Team Leaders (NCAA.org)

Rank	School	G	Attendance	Average
1.	Kentucky	18	405,964	22,554
2.	North Carolina	16	327,953	20,497
3.	Syracuse	22	447,587	20,345
4.	Tennessee	16	324,274	20,267
5.	Louisville	17	331,184	19,481
6.	Maryland	19	341,050	17,950
7.	Wisconsin	18	309,420	17,190
8.	Arkansas	16	274,360	17,148
9.	Indiana	19	320,641	16,876
10.	Memphis	21	351,718	16,748
11.	Illinois	15	249,270	16,618
12.	Ohio St.	20	331,731	16,587
13.	Kansas	20	328,182	16,409
14.	Marquette	17	276,064	16,239
15.	Creighton	18	276,000	15,333
16.	North Carolina St.	16	240,682	15,043
17.	Michigan St.	17	250,903	14,759
18.	New Mexico	18	258,493	14,361
19.	Arizona	17	241,703	14,218
20.	Texas	18	248,673	13,815
21.	BYU	16	216,295	13,518

Rank	School	G	Attendance	Average
22.	Vanderbilt	19	254,945	13,418
23.	Iowa St.	18	239,697	13,317
24.	Georgetown	16	207,286	12,955
25.	Kansas St.	17	212,987	12,529
26.	Oklahoma St.	16	200,056	12,504
27.	Dayton	18	224,623	12,479
28.	Minnesota	17	211,685	12,452
29.	South Carolina	17	209,880	12,346
30.	Purdue	17	209,870	12,345
31.	Wake Forest	17	202,282	11,899
32.	Connecticut	17	202,082	11,887
33.	UNLV	21	249,171	11,865
34.	Virginia	20	234,092	11,705
35.	Pittsburgh	18	197,447	10,969
36.	Florida	21	226,815	10,801
37.	Iowa	18	193,700	10,761
38.	UCLA	18	190,438	10,580
39.	Wichita St.	15	157,170	10,478
40.	Alabama	18	186,640	10,369
41.	Texas A&M	20	206,860	10,343
42.	Nebraska	20	205,722	10,286
43.	Oklahoma	17	174,422	10,260
44.	West Virginia	16	163,315	10,207
45.	Fresno St.	17	173,066	10,180
46.	Michigan	15	150,504	10,034
47.	Xavier	17	170,133	10,008
48.	Utah	15	149,687	9,979
49.	Villanova	15	147,570	9,838
50.	Virginia Tech	17	166,858	9,815
51.	Notre Dame	17	165,337	9,726
52.	Bradley	19	182,392	9,600
53.	Duke	16	149,024	9,314

Rank	School	G	Attendance	Average
54.	DePaul	15	138,927	9,262
55.	Mississippi St.	15	138,789	9,253
56.	Georgia Tech	13	119,483	9,191
57.	Utah St.	17	154,302	9,077
58.	St. Louis	16	141,387	8,837
59.	Washington	19	166,475	8,762
60.	Oregon	15	130,521	8,701
61.	Clemson	16	137,739	8,609
62.	LSU	15	128,469	8,565
63.	Cincinnati	17	145,081	8,534
64.	Providence	15	127,907	8,527
65.	Southern California	15	127,014	8,468
66.	Washington St.	16	131,701	8,231
67.	UTEP	16	130,321	8,145
68.	Missouri	17	137,027	8,060
69.	Penn St.	17	136,693	8,041
70.	Arizona St.	20	160,152	8,008
71.	California	19	150,383	7,915
72.	Georgia	16	125,172	7,823
73.	Florida St.	18	137,508	7,639
74.	Nevada	16	119,488	7,468
75.	Stanford	17	124,621	7,331
76.	Charlotte	16	116,944	7,309
77.	Mississippi	18	131,413	7,301
78.	Baylor	16	116,015	7,251
79.	Seton Hall	17	122,834	7,226
80.	Texas Tech	16	114,615	7,163
81.	San Diego St.	14	94,638	6,760
82.	Old Dominion	17	114,857	6,756
83.	Southern Ill.	16	106,555	6,660
84.	Illinois St.	18	117,293	6,516
85.	George Mason	14	90,920	6,494

Rank	School	G	Attendance	Average
86.	Siena	17	110,012	6,471
87.	Western Ky.	15	95,961	6,397
88.	Missouri St.	16	99,859	6,241
89.	Davidson	14	86,993	6,214
90.	Hawaii	18	111,072	6,171
91.	VCU	14	86,369	6,169
92.	New Mexico St.	20	123,055	6,153
93.	Temple	14	85,637	6,117
94.	Drake	15	90,571	6,038
95.	Gonzaga	14	84,000	6,000
96.	Butler	15	89,169	5,945
97.	St. John's (N.Y.)	16	94,183	5,886
98.	Oral Roberts	13	75,795	5,830
99.	Boston College	19	109,789	5,778
100.	Tulsa	20	115,027	5,751

Division II and III Men's Basketball Attendance Team Leaders (NCAA.org)

Rank	Division II	G	Attendance	Average
1.	Northern St.	18	58,869	3,270
2.	Morehouse	14	42,816	3,058
3.	Elizabeth City St.	12	35,520	2,960
4.	South Dakota	16	46,165	2,885
5.	Augustana (S.D.)	15	40,882	2,725
6.	Central Mo.	15	39,766	2,651
7.	St. Cloud St.	16	41,576	2,598
8.	Winona St.	23	57,490	2,499
9.	Virginia St.	12	29,664	2,472
10.	Washburn	13	31,107	2,392
11.	Emporia St.	14	30,187	2,156
12.	Alas. Anchorage	21	41,894	1,994
13.	Harding	13	25,104	1,931
14.	Southern Ind.	18	33,875	1,881
15.	Minn. St. Mankato	16	29,936	1,871
16.	North Dakota	14	26,122	1,865
17.	Mo. Western St.	14	25,668	1,833
18.	Southwest Minn. St.	14	25,617	1,829
19.	Ky. Wesleyan	17	29,300	1,723
20.	Tarleton St.	19	32,355	1,702
21.	Pittsburg St.	13	20,844	1,603
22.	Gannon	17	26,773	1,574
23.	Grand Valley St.	21	33,020	1,572
24.	Fort Hays St.	16	25,080	1,567
25.	Virginia Union	15	23,519	1,567
26.	Fayetteville St.	11	16,719	1,519
27.	Adams St.	11	16,457	1,496
28.	S.C. Aiken	16	23,667	1,479
29.	California (Pa.)	17	23,633	1,390
30.	Mo. Southern St.	14	19,298	1,378

Rank	Division III	G/S	Attendance	Average
1.	Hope	17	51,278	3,016
2.	Wooster	15	24,318	1,621
3.	Ill. Wesleyan	11	16,350	1,486
4.	Buena Vista	13	18,525	1,425
5.	Calvin	13	17,856	1,373
6.	Wis.-Stevens Point	14	18,901	1,350
7.	Keene St.	13	17,132	1,317
8.	Mass.-Dartmouth	17	22,375	1,316
9.	Lincoln (Pa.)	8	10,411	1,301
10.	Puget Sound	12	14,580	1,215
11.	Capital	15	18,221	1,214
12.	Messiah	11	13,213	1,201
13.	Augustana (Ill.)	16	16,999	1,062
14.	Rochester (N.Y.)	16	16,508	1,031
15.	York (Pa.)	14	14,296	1,021
16.	Chris. Newport	15	15,162	1,010
17.	Maryville (Tenn.)	13	12,981	998
18.	Wheaton (Ill.)	10	9,955	995
19.	New York U.	16	15,539	971
20.	Whitworth	11	10,495	954
21.	Mississippi Col.	12	11,411	950
22.	St. John's (Minn.)	11	10,309	937
23.	Pomona-Pitzer	11	10,246	931
24.	Washington-St. Louis	14	13,013	929
25.	Wartburg	13	11,959	919
26.	Brandeis	14	12,850	917
27.	Howard Payne	12	10,612	884
28.	Muskingum	12	10,586	882
29.	Otterbein	11	9,593	872
30.	Mary Hardin-Baylor	16	13,675	85

GLOSSARY

AAU sports: A multi-sport organization dedicated to the promotion and development of amateur sports and physical fitness programs. The AAU currently operates as a voluntary organization largely promoting youth sports.

Athletic conference: A collection of sports teams, playing competitively against each other at the collegiate or high school level. In many cases conferences are subdivided into smaller and smaller divisions, with the best teams competing at successively higher levels.

Atlantic Coast Conference (ACC): A collegiate athletic league in the United States. Founded in 1953, the ACC's twelve-member universities compete in twenty sports in the NCAA's Division I. Current members include Boston College, Clemson University, Duke University, Florida State University, Georgia Tech, University of Maryland, University of Miami, University of North Carolina at Chapel Hill, North Carolina State University, University of Virginia, Virginia Tech, and Wake Forest University.

Big Ten Conference: The oldest Division I college athletic conference in the United States. Its eleven-member institutions are located primarily in the Midwestern United States, stretching from Iowa and Minnesota in the west to Pennsylvania in the east. Current members include University of Illinois, Indiana University, University of Iowa, University of Michigan, Michigan State University, University of Minnesota, Northwestern University, Ohio State University, Penn State University, Purdue University, and University of Wisconsin.

Big Twelve Conference: A college athletic conference of twelve schools located mostly in the central United States. It participates in the NCAA's Division I in athletic competitions. Members are split between the North and South divisions. Current members of the North division include Iowa State University, Kansas State University, University of Colorado, University of Kansas, University of Missouri, and University of Nebraska. Current members of the South division include Baylor University, Oklahoma State University, Texas A&M University, Texas Tech University, University of Oklahoma, and the University of Texas.

Club sports/club teams: Organized sports activity that occurs outside of the varsity team that is sponsored by the school. In the context of this book, it refers to competition that is completely outside of the high school environment. Club sports can also be sponsored within a high school or university where participants can learn skills and engage in competition, but are not part of organized varsity competition.

Division I (D-I): The highest level of intercollegiate athletics sanctioned by the National Collegiate Athletic Association in the United States. D-I schools are the major collegiate athletic powers, with larger budgets, more elaborate facilities, and higher numbers of athletic scholarships. Currently, Division I has about 333 institutions plus 5 going through the Reclassification Period.

Division II (D-II): An intermediate-level division of competition in the National Collegiate Athletic Association. It offers an alternative to both the highly competitive (and highly expensive) level of intercollegiate sports offered in NCAA Division I and to the non-scholarship level offered in Division III. Division II schools tend to be smaller public universities and many private institutions. Athletic scholarships are offered in most sponsored sports at most institutions, but with more stringent limits as to the numbers offered in any one sport than at the Division I level. Currently Division II has about 294 institutions.

Division III (D-III): A division of the National Collegiate Athletic Association of the United States. The division consists of colleges and universities that choose not to offer athletically related financial aid (athletic scholarships) to their student-athletes. There are 444 member institutions (both full and provisional), making Division III the largest of the three divisions sanctioned by the National Collegiate Athletic Association. D-III schools range in size from less than 500 to over 10,000 students. D-III schools compete in athletics as a non-revenue-making, extracurricular activity for students.

Early action: A type of early admissions process for admission to colleges and universities in the United States. Unlike the regular admissions process, early action usually requires students to submit an application by November 1 of their senior year of high school instead of January 1. Students are notified of the school's decision by mid-December instead of April 1. Early action allows candidates to decline the offer if accepted. There are two types of early action programs: restrictive early action and non-restrictive early action. Restrictive EA allows candidates to apply to only one early action institution and to no institutions early decision, while, as the name implies, there are no such restrictions on non-restrictive early action. Regardless, the applicant is still permitted to reject any offer of admission in both types of early action.

Early decision: A common early admission policy used in college admissions in the United States for admitting freshmen to undergraduate programs. It is used to indicate to the university or college that the candidate considers that institution to be his or her top choice. Candidates applying early decision typically submit their applications by the end of October of their senior year of high school and receive a decision in mid-December. In contrast, students applying regular decision typically must submit their applications by January 1 and receive their admissions decision by April 1. Early decision constitutes a binding commitment to enroll; that is, if offered admission under an early decision program the candidate must withdraw all other applications to other institutions and enroll at that institution. Furthermore, early decision programs limit applicants to filing one early application.

Elite athlete: While there is no specific criteria for being considered an elite athlete, the use of the term in this book is meant to refer to those athletes selected or regarded as the best, most accomplished, most powerful, and most likely to continue to professional ranks within their sport. It is typically less than 5 percent of those competing in an NCAA-sanctioned program.

Impact athlete: An athlete whose performance has a distinct and measurable impact on his or her team's overall success.

Intramural sports: Recreational sports organized within schools that are conducted between members of the same school as opposed to varsity teams who compete with other schools. Oftentimes students administer these programs under the supervision of a faculty sponsor or intramural coordinator. The competitive nature of the events is characterized as informal, but the intensity can be very high.

Ivy League: An athletic conference comprising eight private institutions of higher education located in the Northeastern United States. It participates in the NCAA's Division I in athletic competitions. The use of the phrase Ivy League is no longer limited to athletics, and now represents an educational philosophy of academic excellence, selectivity in admissions, and a reputation for social elitism. Current members include Harvard University, Yale University, University of Pennsylvania, Cornell University, Princeton University, Dartmouth College, Brown University, and Columbia University.

NCAA sports: The National Collegiate Athletic Association is a voluntary association of about 1,200 institutions, conferences, organizations, and individuals that organizes the athletic programs of many colleges and universities in the United States. The NCAA is the largest collegiate athletic organization in the world, and because of the great popularity of college sports among spectators in the United States, it is far more prominent than most national college sports bodies in other countries.

NCAA Clearinghouse (also known as the NCAA Initial Eligibility Center): The Clearinghouse processes academic qualifications for all prospective Division I and Division II athletes and determines whether they are eligible to compete.

Pacific Ten Conference (also known as the Pac-10): A college athletic conference that operates in the western United States. It participates in the NCAA Division I in athletic competitions. Current members include University of Arizona, Arizona State University, University of California at Berkeley, University of Oregon, Oregon State University, Stanford University, University of California at Los Angeles, University of Southern California, University of Washington, and Washington State University.

Patriot League: A college athletic conference that operates in the northeastern United States. It participates in the NCAA's Division I in athletic competitions. Patriot League members are schools with very strong academic reputations that adhere strongly to the ideal of the "scholar-athlete," with the emphasis on "scholar." Out-of-league play for Patriot League schools is typically with members of the Ivy League, which follow similar philosophies regarding academics and athletics. Current members include American University, Bucknell University, Colgate University, College of the Holy Cross, Lafayette College, Lehigh University, United States Military Academy (Army), and United States Naval Academy (Navy).

Prospect camps or camps: Camps that are designed for players who are interested in developing skills to pursue their sport at the collegiate level. These are typically, but not always, held in the summer and are often hosted by college coaches at their respective campuses. They are called prospect camps because the coaches are looking for future prospects for their collegiate programs.

Redshirt: When a college athlete is withdrawn from college sporting events during one year in order to develop skills and extend the period of playing eligibility by a further year at this level of competition. The term "redshirt" comes from the red shirts worn by such athletes in practices with regular team members.

Regular decision: Refers to the traditional college admissions process where applications are due by January 1 of a student's senior year of high school, and decision letters are usually mailed to applicants in the spring, typically around April 1. Students may be accepted to the institution, rejected outright, or waitlisted. Waitlisted students may be later admitted if another student who was admitted decides not to attend the college or university.

Showcases: Typically one- to three-day events that provide an opportunity for athletes to "showcase" their skills in front of college coaches and scouts, gaining maximum exposure. Participants may be evaluated for both specific individual skills and overall game performance. It is not necessary to be part of a team to participate in showcase events.

Southeastern Conference (SEC): A college athletic conference headquartered in Birmingham, Alabama, which operates in the southeastern part of the United States and participates in the NCAA's Division I in athletic competitions. Members of the eastern division include the University of Florida, University of Georgia, University of Kentucky, University of South Carolina, University of Tennessee, and Vanderbilt University. Members of the western division include the University of Alabama, University of Arkansas, Auburn University, Louisiana State University, University of Mississippi, and Mississippi State University.

Walk-on: An athlete who becomes part of a team without being actively recruited beforehand or awarded an athletic scholarship. Often these athletes are relegated to the scout team, and may not even be played on the official depth chart or traveling team. In some instances, a college coach/recruiter may designate an athlete as a "preferred walk-on" during the scouting process. In this situation, the athlete is assured a spot on the team; however, the coach is unable or unwilling to offer a scholarship.

REFERENCES

Books

Britz, Patrick and Alexandra Powe Allred. *Athletic Scholarships for Dummies.* Hoboken, N.J.: Wiley Publishing, Inc., 2006.

Buyers, Colleen and Jordan Goldman, eds. *The Definitive Guide to America's Top 100 Schools Written by the Real Experts—The Students Who Attend Them.* New York: Penguin Books, 2005.

Coburn, Karen Levin and Treeger, Madge Lawrence. *Letting Go: A Parents' Guide to Understanding the College Years.* 5th ed. New York, NY: Harper Collins, 2009.

College Guide 2009: A Guide to Over 380 Colleges and Unlimited Paths to your Future. New York: Kaplan Publishing, 2008.

College Handbook 2009. 46th ed. Edited by Tom Vandenberg. New York: College Board, 2008.

Fiske, Edward with Robert Logue. *Fiske Guide to Colleges 2009.* 25th ed. Naperville, IL: Sourcebooks, Inc., 2008.

Four-Year Colleges 2009 (Peterson's Four-Year Colleges). 39th ed. Edited by Fern Oram. Lawrenceville, NJ: Peterson's, 2008.

Franek, Robert, Tom Meltzer, Christopher Maier, Erik Olson, Carson Brown, Julie Doherty, Adam O. Davis, and Eric Owens. *The Best 368 Colleges—The Smart Student's Guide to Colleges:* 2009 Edition. New York: Random House, 2008.

Getting Financial Aid 2009. New York: The College Board, 2008.

Peterson's Scholarships, Grants & Prizes 2009. 13th ed. Lawrenceville, NJ: Peterson's Nelnet Co., 2008.

Peterson's Sports Scholarships & College Athletic Programs. 5th ed. Edited by Joe Krawowski. Lawrenceville, NJ: Thomson Peterson's, 2004.

Princeton Review Complete Book of Colleges 2009 Edition. New York: Random House, 2008.

Scholarship Handbook 2009. 12th ed. Edited by Tom Vandenberg. New York: The College Board, 2008.

The High School Athlete's Guide to College Sports—How to Market Yourself to the School of Your Dreams. College Bound Sports. Lanham, MD: First Taylor Trade Publishing, 2005.

The Insider's Guide to the Colleges, 2009: Students on Campus Tell You What You Really Want to Know. 35th ed. Compiled and edited by the Yale Daily News Staff. New York: St. Martin's Griffin, 2008.

U.S. News Ultimate College Guide 2008. 5th ed. Edited by Anne McGrath. Naperville, IL: Sourcebooks, Inc., 2007.

Websites

www.NCAA.org
(Contains a link to NCAA.com)—everything about specific sports and schools across D-I, D-II, and D-III, rules, advice for student-athletes, past statistics, you name it

www.NCAAstudent.org
Download the guide for the college-bound student-athlete—it's full of great information

www.NAIA.org
National Association of Intercollegiate Athletics

www.NJCAA.org
National Junior College Athletic Association

www.Petersons.com
Includes a good school selection tool and scholarship database

www.collegeboard.com
Includes a good selection tool

www.USNews.com
Yearly reviews of America's best colleges

www.ncaaclearinghouse.net
Information and registration for the NCAA Clearinghouse for D-I and D-II athletes

www.FastWeb.com
Extensive scholarship database including both institutional scholarships and scholarships available from outside sources

www.D3hoops.com
Everything about D-III basketball

www.D3football.com
Everything about D-III football

www.D3baseball.com
Everything about D-III baseball

www.D3soccer.com
Everything about D-III soccer

www.national-letter.org
Information about the national letter of intent for scholarship athletes

www.masseyratings.com.
Ratings for twelve sports, both genders, and all levels including high school, college, and pro

INDEX

A

AAU. *See* Amateur Athletic Union (AAU)
academic scholarships. *See* merit
    (academic) scholarships
academic standards
    ACT scores, 50–53
    athletic priority *vs.*, 61–62
    average, 55
    competitive, 175
    D-I schools, 49–52
    D-II schools, 49–52
    D-III coaches and, 54–56
    D-III schools, 50, 52–54, 56, 63–64
    grade point average (GPA), 51, 53, 55
    graduation rates by division and sport,
        57–58
    Ivy League, 49, 52, 54, 64
    NCAA Clearinghouse standards, 49–50,
        52, 54, 59
    Patriot League, 49, 64
    questions, academic *vs.* athletic priority,
        64–65
    SAT scores, 50–53
academic standing, improving, 35
ACC. *See* Atlantic Coast (ACC)
ACT scores, 50–52
Akita, James, 78, 87
Amateur Athletic Union (AAU)
    basketball, 30, 62, 110
    coaches, 36, 107, 110
    competition, 109
    expectations for, 128–31
    exposure events, 100–101
    leagues, 98
    player, 29
    showcase events, 127
    sports, 109, 130, 197
    statistics, 37
    teams, 100, 125, 129–30
archery, 75
athletic conferences, 189–90, 197
    athletic scholarships. *See also*
        community-service-based
        scholarships; merit (academic)
        scholarships; need-based
        scholarships
    average NCAA, 76–77
    college paid by, 17
    NCAA allotment of, 75
    NCAA Division I, 29

NCAA Division I *vs.* Division III, 86–87
NCAA Division II, 31
offers made to children, 111
opportunity, 73–77
parent's expectations, 129–30
partial, 31, 33, 74, 76
Peterson's Sports Scholarships & College
    Athletic Programs, 116, 201
by sport, 75
total dollars by four-year colleges, 81
women's, 77
athletic skill assessment
    AAU/club team coaches, 36
    AAU/club team statistics, 37
    athletic websites at colleges, 36, 38–39,
        41, 202
    child's frame of reference, 28
    by college coaches, 36
    high school seniors on college team,
        38–39, 41
    high school statistics, 37
    high school team experience, 38
    motivation, parent's *vs.* child's, 45
    non-high school events, 37, 41
    parent's assessment, 21–23, 27, 40–41
    parent's objectivity, 40
    by private trainers, 36
    role on team, perceived, 43–47
    skill level and right program, 29
    website research, 38–39, 41
    wrong assessment, downside of, 40–41
Atlantic Coast Conference (ACC), 92, 197

B

backup plan, 40, 71, 181–83
badminton, 75, 114
Bailey, Pat, 18, 40
baseball, 18, 20, 28, 39–40, 202
Bellantoni, Roc, 19, 164
bench warmer, 45–46
Big East, 92
big name school, 14
Big Ten Conference, 92, 197
Big Twelve Conference, 92, 197
bowling, 75, 114
bragging rights, 14, 17
Brand, Myles, 84–85
Browning, John, 56
Bryant, Amy, 86
Butler University, 21, 165

C

campus visit, 98, 122, 141–43, 147–59
Carnegie Mellon University, 46, 77, 137, 157
child. *See also* parent-child team
    athletic scholarships, direct offers by
        coaches, 111
    athletic skill assessment, 28
    athletic talent, coach's view, 123–24
    athletic talent, parent's assessment,
        21–23, 27, 40–41, 122–23
    burn-out, 129
    coaches access to, 110–11
    disillusionment and frustration, 18
    motivation of, 45
    parent's dialogue with, 13
    point of view, right to personal, 13
    questions for, 158
    with team members, 150–51
Claremont-Mudd-Scripps Athletics, 46, 140
club
    coaches, 107, 110
    exposure events, 100–101
    off-season, 125
    showcase events, 127
    sports/club teams, 129–30, 197
    team statistics, 37
    teams, expectations for, 128–31
coaches
    academic standards and D-III, 54–56
    access to child, 110–11
    admission decisions and, 54–56
    admissions office and, 56–57
    Amateur Athletic Union, 36, 107, 110
    child's athletic skill assessment and
        AAU/club, 36
    child's athletic skill assessment and
        college, 36
    child's compatibility with the, 145–47
    child's talent, assessment of, 123–24
    club, 107, 110
    Division III, 32, 54–56, 108, 142
    high school, 36–37, 101, 107–10, 116,
        121, 124, 129, 137
    initiating contact with, 97
    marketing your child to, 120–22
    questions for, 64–65, 144–45, 154–55
    recruiting style of, 147–48
college assessment
    appeal of school without sport, 91–92
    campus life, 68
    career-ending injury and, 91, 95
    culture of school, 70
    D-III conference ranking, 94
    D-III school ranking, 93–94
    fan support, 94–95
    financial aid availability, 70
    fraternities and sororities, 70
    home, proximity to, 68
    non-varsity sports, 70
    program, comfort with, 92–93
    program of study, 69
    public *vs.* private, 69
    ranking of school for sports, 93
    religious affiliation, 69
    setting (urban *vs.* rural), 67
    size of college, 67
    sports program as a spectator, 69–70
    study abroad program, 70
    weather, 69
    winning record of school, 93
college athletics
    appeal of, 17
    athletic skill, 19–20
    D-III philosophy, 32
    expectations, 19
    priorities, athletics *vs.* academics, 61–64
    suitability of, 22
College of Wooster, 71
Colorado College, 32
community service, 77, 86–87
community-service-based scholarships, 86.
    See also athletic scholarships
Connell, Kathleen, 85
Cosmiano, Peter, 109
cross-country, 53–54, 64, 114, 146, 157, 165

D

D-I. *See* Division I (D-I)
D-II. *See* Division II (D-II)
D-III. *See* Division III (D-III)
Davis, Sarah, 71
decision making
    athletic ability, differences in, 165
    athletic scholarship, D-I *vs.* D-II, 171–72
    athletic scholarship, without, 173
    backup plan, 40, 71, 181–83
    considerations, other, 165–66
    between D-I or D-II and D-III, 163–64
    D-I *vs.* D-III, comparing, 166
    D-III schools, choosing between, 167–69
    decision, telling coaches the, 178–79
    early decision, 174–75
    early decision, downside to, 175–76
    early decision and financial package, 177–78
    public *vs.* private schools, 69, 166–67
    schools, comparing, 168–69
    selection criteria, 168
    time commitment, 164–65
diving, 75, 114, 148, 153
Division I (D-I). *See also* NCAA
    about, 198
    academic standards, 49–52

athletic ability, 165
athletic scholarships, 29, 73–75, 86–87,
 171–72
familiarity, 30
fan support, 94–95
graduation rates, 57–58
NCAA Basketball attendance (2008),
 191–94
NCAA Clearinghouse standards, 50
NCAA guidelines, 164
status, 29–30
transition to the pros, 30
Division II (D-II)
 about, 198
 academic standards, 49–52
 athletic scholarship/financial need, 31
 athletic scholarships, 31, 73–75, 171–72
 fan support, 94–95
 graduation rates, 57–58
 NCAA Basketball attendance (2008), 195–96
 NCAA Clearinghouse standards, 50
Division III (D-III)
 about, 198
 academic standards, 52–54, 56, 63–64
 academic standards and coaches, 54–56
 athletic ability, 165
 athletic/academic balance, 32–33
 coaches, 32, 108, 142
 conferences and websites, 189–90
 fan support, 94–95
 financial aid, 73, 77–78, 81–82
 financial need, 31, 33
 graduation rates, 57–58
 high-impact player, 165
 merit (academic) scholarships, 78–79,
  84–86
 NCAA Basketball attendance (2008),
  195–96
 NCAA Clearinghouse standards, 52
Drake, Diane, 19, 165
Duke University, 49

E
early action, 173, 176, 198
early admissions programs, 176
early decision, 174–78, 198
Eastern Illinois University, 19, 164
Eckenrode, Megan, 32
elite athlete, 30, 61, 98, 122–23, 199
elite events, 30
Elmhurst College, 78, 87
Emory University, 56, 86, 137
equestrian, 75
equivalency sports, 76
"Expectations Lose to Reality of Sports
 Scholarships" (Brand), 84–85

extracurricular activities, 87–88, 198

F
Facebook, 111
FAFSA. *See* Federal Student Aid (FAFSA)
fan support, 94–95
FastWeb.com, 86
Federal Student Aid (FAFSA), 101
fencing, 75, 114
field hockey, 32, 120, 128, 140
financial constraints, 14, 175. *See also*
 money concerns
football, 19–21, 28, 39, 77, 148, 157, 164, 202
Franklin and Marshall College, 54, 120, 140
freshman year, 68, 92, 97, 99–100, 154, 177
Frostburg State University, 9, 63, 83–84, 147

G
George Mason University, 18–19, 165
golf, 19, 22, 75, 114, 153
grade point average (GPA)
 academic (merit) grants and, 80–81
 academic standards, 51, 53, 55
 raising score, 97
graduation rates, 57–58, 64, 154
Griffiths, Charles, 140
gymnastics, 75–76, 114

H
Harvard University, 84, 176
Haverford College, 84
headcount sports, 76
high school
 academic grades, 75
 athletic ability, 123
 athletic conference, 197
 basketball, 56, 74, 110
 best players, 28
 choice, 62
 coaches, 36–37, 101, 107–10, 116, 121,
  124, 129, 137
 competition, 109
 Division I scholarship, 30
 football team, 44, 78
 friends, access to, 168
 lacrosse, 122
 leadership and commitment, 89
 letters of recommendation, 101
 NCAA Clearinghouse standards, 50, 100
 prep school after, 35
 recruitment process in, 97–98
 senior, and state tournament, 43
 seniors on college team, 38–39, 41
 seniors' prospecting letters, 136
 soccer, 147
 sports *vs.* college sports, 22

statistics, 36–37, 41
team experience, 19, 28, 35–38, 88
team role *vs.* Club/AAU teams, 129
transcript, 52
United States statistics, 28
videotape games, 119, 140
volleyball, 92
hockey, 75, 114
Hofstra University, 21, 164
humor, 14–15

I
ice hockey, 28, 39, 75, 114
Illinois Wesleyan, 83
impact athlete, 45, 47, 199
The Insider's Guide to the Colleges, 95
intramural sports, 20, 70, 199
Ivy League, 49, 52, 64, 84, 199

J
Johns Hopkins University, 99, 148, 175
junior college, 33–34, 41, 49, 99, 138, 172, 202
junior year, 30, 34, 36, 38, 50, 53, 97–101,
      116, 120, 126–27, 143, 152–53

K
Keeping Score
    academic standards, 59
    athletic skill assessment, 41
    backup plan, 183
    campus visit, 159
    college sport decision, 23
    deciding which offer is best, 169
    decision, making the final, 180
    marketing your child, 131, 148
    money concerns, 89
    non-athletic college priorities, 71
    parent-child team, 15
    priorities, athletic *vs.* academic, 66
    recruiting process, starting the, 103
    who does what, 107
Keith, Steven, 146, 165
Kendrick, Pat, 18
Kennedy, George, 148
Kilburn-Steveskey, Krista, 21, 164
Kinney, Joe, 20

L
Lackner, Richard, 77, 157
lacrosse, 40, 68, 75, 109, 114, 121–22
Lafayette College, 20
leadership skills, 88–89, 114, 119
Liskevych, Terry, 148

M
Macdonald, Geoff, 22
Marist College, 20–21

marketing your child. *See also* recruitment
      process
AAU and club teams, expectations for,
      128–31
alternatives to doing it yourself, 127–28
athletic programs, insights about, 138–39
athletic scholarship expectations, 129–30
campus, when to visit, 152–53
campus tour, 151–52
campus visit, questions for coaching
      staff, 154–55
campus visit, questions for team
      members, 155
campus visit, what happens during, 149–50
campus visit and expectation to play,
      156–57
campus visit and parents, 140–43
child burn-out, 129
child with team members, 150–51
child's talent, coach's view, 123–24
child's talent, parent's view, 122–23
coach, compatibility with the, 145–47
to coaches, 120–22
coaches, recruiting style of, 147–48
cover letter, 117
hearing what you want to hear, 144
individual sports, objective, 114–15
individual sports, subjective, 114
interest, expressing lack of, 139–40
letters, first, 135–37
letters, follow-up, 137–39
limits, setting, 140
marketing strategy #1, 115
marketing strategy #2, 115–24
marketing strategy #3, 124
marketing strategy #4, 125–27
off-season club, 125
prospect camps, 125–27
questions for coaching staff, 144–45
questions for the child, 158
resume, 118, 127
in senior year, 99
showcase events, 125
social networking on Internet, 111–12
starting, 97–99
team sports, 114
timeline, ideal, 100–101
videotaping athletic events, 98, 111, 114,
      119–20, 127–28, 140
Martin, Jay, 144
McLaughlin, Brian, 153
men's. *See also* women's
    basketball, 21, 32, 39, 165
    cross country, 78, 87, 99
    golf, 19, 22
    soccer, 76, 144, 175
    tennis, 56, 63

track and field, 78, 87, 99
merit (academic) scholarships. *See also*
    athletic scholarships
    comparisons by school, 82–84
    Division III, 78–79, 84–86
Miller, Rob, 19, 22
Mississippi College, 109
Mohr, Steven, 148
money concerns. *See also* academic
    standards; athletic scholarships;
    merit (academic) scholarships
    athletic scholarship, average NCAA, 76–77
    athletic scholarship, partial, 31, 33, 74, 76
    athletic scholarship, women's, 77
    athletic scholarship by sport, 75
    athletic scholarship opportunity, 73–77
    D-II financial need, 31
    D-III financial aid, 73, 77–78, 81–82
    financial aid availability, 70
    financial package and early decision,
        177–78
    Ivy League schools, 84
    merit (academic) grants and GPA, 80–81
    merit (academic) scholarship, 78–79, 82–86
    scholarship dollars at four-year colleges,
        81
    scholarships, community-service-based, 86
    scholarships, D-I *vs.* D-III, 86–87
    scholarships, need-based, 84, 86
Montclair State University, 153
MySpace, 111

N
NAIA. *See* National Association of
    Intercollegiate Athletics (NAIA)
National Association of Intercollegiate
    Athletics (NAIA), 29, 33
National Junior College Athletic Association
    (NJCAA), 29
national letter of intent, 171–72, 202
national media coverage, 165
NCAA (National Collegiate Athletic
    Association). *See also* Division I
    (D-I); Division II (D-II); Division III
    (D-III)
    athletic scholarship, average, 76–77
    athletic scholarship allotment, 75
    basketball attendance (2008), 191–96
    Clearinghouse Eligibility Center standards,
        34–35, 49–50, 52, 54, 59, 100, 199
    Clearinghouse registration, 97
    freshman roster positions available, 28
    Initial Eligibility Center, 199
    sports, 199
NCAAclearinghouse.net, 52, 101
NCAA.org, 57, 94
NCAAstudent.org, 52

need-based scholarships, 84, 86. *See also*
    athletic scholarships
NJCAA. *See* National Junior College Athletic
    Association (NJCAA)
non-high school events, 36–37, 41, 127
Northwestern University, 49

O
off-season
    breaks, 154
    clubs, 125
    competitions, 8, 110
    jobs, 164
    teams, 98
    tournaments, 140
    training, 18, 21, 64
Ohio Wesleyan University, 144
Olswanger, Aaron, 64
Oregon State University, 18, 40, 148

P
Pacific Ten Conference (Pac-10), 92, 199
Parady, James, 20–21
parent-child team. *See also* child
    agendas, mismatched, 14
    athletic scholarships, parent's
        expectations, 129–30
    campus visit, 140–43
    campus visit and expectation to play,
        156–57
    child, parent's dialogue with, 13
    child's athletic talent, parent's
        assessment, 21–23, 27, 40–41, 122–23
    child's disillusionment and frustration, 18
    child's point of view, 13
    motivation, parent's *vs.* child's, 45, 62
    parent's conditions, 14
    parent's control, 15
    parent's objectivity, 40
    parent's over-involvement, 21–23
    recruiting process, 13, 107–9
parent's footsteps, walking in, 14
Parker, Brian, 9, 147
Partee, Andy, 32
partial athletic scholarship, 31, 33, 74, 76
Patriot League, 49, 64, 199
Pennington, Bill, 63, 76–77, 130
Peterson's Four-Year Colleges, 82–83
*Peterson's Scholarships, Grants & Prizes
    2009,* 201
*Peterson's Sports Scholarships & College
    Athletic Programs,* 116, 201
Petersons.com, 86
Pomona College, 84–85
practice player, 45–46
Prep School, 35
Princeton Review, 52

Princeton University, 176
private trainers, 36
pro team, 52
professional agent, 52
professional career in sports, 17
prospect camps, 101, 124–27, 200
psychological strength, 19
public *vs.* private schools, 69, 166–67
Purdue University, 19, 22

Q

questions
    for the child, 158
    for coaches, 64–65, 144–45, 154–55
    for players, 65
    priority, academic *vs.* athletic, 64–65
    for team members, 155

R

recruiters, 98, 113, 128, 140
recruiting style of coaches, 147–48
recruitment process. *See also* marketing
        your child
    coaches' access to children, 110–11
    college recruitment, changes in, 109–10
    in high school, 97–98
    NCAA clearinghouse.net, 52, 101
    responsibilities, parent-child, 13, 107–9
    scholarship offers made to children, 111
redshirt, 154, 200
references, 201–2
regular decision, 56, 173–74, 177–78, 200
romantic relationships, 20
rowing, 54
rugby, 75

S

Salem State College, 41, 144
Sanchez, Keri, 46
Santa Clara University, 19, 22
scholar-athlete, 199
scholarships, community-service-based, 86
scholarships, need-based, 84, 86
Schwarz, Dr. Toby C., 157
SEC. *See* Southeastern Conference (SEC)
Seidl, Gerri, 46, 137
Shea, Timothy, 41, 144
showcase events, 125, 127, 200
Siqueiros, Penny, 137
Smith, Matt, 175
Soboti, Suzette, 109
soccer, 28, 39, 43, 46, 75–76, 85, 93, 114, 121,
        128, 130, 144, 147, 153, 165, 175, 202
social networking, 111–12
softball, 75, 114, 137
sophomore year, 100
Southeastern Conference (SEC), 92, 200

Stanford University, 49
Stevens, Brad, 21, 165
stretch schools, 59
Students' Guide to Colleges: The Definitive
        Guide to America's Top 100 Schools, 94
study abroad programs, 70
Swarthmore College, 84
swimming, 140, 148, 153
Swink, Stuart, 63

T

team roster, 38
television coverage, 165
tennis, 22, 56, 63, 75–76, 86, 114
time management, 18–19
track and field, 75–76, 78, 87, 114, 153, 157
Trinity University, 148
trophy kids, 21

U

UC Berkeley University, 49
UCLA University, 49
University of Pennsylvania, 84
University of Redlands, 64, 109
University of Virginia, 176

V

Van Allen, Bobby, 99
Vanderbilt University, 22, 146, 165
volleyball, 18, 71, 75–76, 92, 109, 114, 121,
        128, 139, 142, 146

W

walk-on, 76, 122, 144, 146, 165, 173, 183, 200
Walkenbach, Elizabeth, 120, 140
water polo, 75, 114, 121–22
websites, 202
Whitworth University, 157
Williams College, 83
Wolter, Claus, 54
women's. *See also* men's basketball, 21, 39,
        41, 46, 85, 137, 144, 164
    cross country, 99
    field hockey, 32
    graduation rates, 57–58
    lacrosse, 109
    soccer, 9, 19, 46, 85, 109, 147, 165
    swimming, 19, 22
    tennis, 22, 63, 86
    track and field, 99
    volleyball, 18, 148
wrestling, 75, 114
Wright-Eger, Catherine, 19, 22

Y

Yale University, 84
York College, 32